TOP 10
CALIFORNIA
WINE COUNTRY

CHRISTOPHER P. BAKER

EYEWITNESS TRAVEL

Left **Napa Valley Wine Train** Right **Canoeing on the Russian River**

LONDON, NEW YORK,
MELBOURNE, MUNICH AND DELHI
www.dk.com

Printed and bound in China by
South China Printing Co. Ltd.

First American Edition, 2012

14 15 16 17 10 9 8 7 6 5 4 3 2 1

Published in the United States by
DK Publishing, 345 Hudson Street,
New York, New York 10014

**Copyright 2012, 2014 © Dorling
Kindersley Limited, London
A Penguin Random House Company**

Published in Great Britain
by Dorling Kindersley Limited

ISSN 1479-344X
ISBN 978 1 4654 1045 0

A catalog record for this book is available from
the Library of Congress.

Within each Top 10 list in this book, no hierarchy
of quality or popularity is implied. All 10 are, in
the editor's opinion, of roughly equal merit.

Contents

California Wine Country's Top 10

Left **Sebastiani Vineyards** Center **Gloria Ferrer Caves and Vineyards** Right **Church of One Tree**

Left **Grape harvesting at The Hess Collection** Right **Restaurant, Francis Ford Coppola Winery**

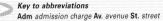

Key to abbreviations
Adm *admission charge* **Av.** *avenue* **St.** *street*

CALIFORNIA WINE COUNTRY'S TOP 10

⊤⦿P10 Highlights

The warm, sheltered valleys north of San Francisco, popularly known as Wine Country, offer amazing diversity due to their varied terrain and microclimates. The wineries here produce excellent wines, and many of them even house art galleries and museums. Add to that historic towns with Victorian architecture; recreational activities such as hot-air ballooning and canoeing; plus excellent spas, world-class dining, and fabulous accommodations, and it is easy to understand why Wine Country is one of California's most popular regions.

The Hess Collection
Tucked amid the slopes of Mount Veeder, this winery is renowned as much for its contemporary art collection as for its quality wines *(see pp8–9)*.

Napa Valley Wine Train
A leisurely sightseeing tour with lunch or dinner aboard this restored historic train with Pullman cars is a relaxing and romantic way to see the Napa Valley end to end *(see pp12–13)*.

Calistoga
Full of historic charm, this town at the northern gateway to Napa Valley is famous for a geyser and its thermal springs and spas *(see pp14–15)*.

Culinary Institute of America
Housed in a landmark winery, the Culinary Institute hosts cooking and wine-tasting classes plus lectures, and has museum exhibits as well as impressive gardens to visit *(see pp16–17)*.

Preceding pages **Hot-air ballooning, Napa Valley**

The Silverado Trail
This scenic highway runs along the tranquil east side of the Napa Valley and is a popular cycling route. It is lined with more than 40 wineries *(see pp18–19)*.

Sonoma State Historic Park
At the heart of Sonoma town, this park preserves many buildings from California's early capital city laid out in traditional Mexican fashion, including Mission San Francisco Solano *(see pp20–21)*.

Santa Rosa
The largest city in Wine Country, Santa Rosa has museums, a restored historic district, and many venues attractive to children including the Charles M. Schulz Museum *(see pp24–5)*.

Aetna Springs
Pope Valley
Calistoga
Angwin
Deer Park
Culinary Institute of America
St. Helena
Zinfandel
Lake Hennessey (128)
Sugarloaf Ridge State Park
Kenwood
The Silverado Trail
Yountville
Napa
The Hess Collection
Oak Knoll
Salvador
Vichy Springs
Ellen
Eldridge
Union
Sonoma State Historic Park
Napa Valley Wine Train
El Verano
Sonoma
Napa

20 ┌─────── miles ┐ 0 ├ km ┐ 20

Russian River
A center for adventures, such as canoeing and fishing, this region appeals for its redwood parks and riverside lodges. The Russian River Jazz and Blues Festival is world-renowned *(see pp26–7)*.

Alexander Valley
The valley's warm climate and alluvial soils produce voluptuous wines. It is home to some of the most highly regarded wineries in Wine Country, as well as the delightful city of Healdsburg *(see pp28–9)*.

Francis Ford Coppola Winery
Decidedly diverse and family-friendly, the Francis Ford Coppola Winery has a movie gallery, an amphitheater, swimming pools, and a gourmet restaurant *(see pp30–31)*.

TOP 10 The Hess Collection

Reached via a winding road up the flank of Mount Veeder and through a redwood forest, this mountain estate is known for its contemporary art collection. Displayed in a two-story gallery, the international collection includes works by European artists as well as renowned masters, and is considered one of the finest in California. The Hess Collection's winery makes use of sustainable techniques for the production of wine and offers opportunities for wine tasting during tours. The estate's landscaped garden, studded with sculptures, has a wild and natural aesthetic.

Barrel room, The Hess Collection

🕐 For the most in-depth knowledge, book the Wine Education Tour & Tasting Experience, which takes participants into the fermentation and barrel rooms, followed by a tasting tutorial in the executive dining room. Check the website for dates.

☁ Check the weather forecast before booking the Wine & Cheese Pairing Tour, hosted in the garden courtyard, which is weather permitting.

• Map L4; 4411 Redwood Rd., Napa, 94558; 707 255 1144; Open 10am–5:30pm; Free winery and museum tour; $15 for wine-tasting; Specialized tasting events and tours for a fee by advance reservation; www. hesscollection.com

Top 10 Features

1. The Winery
2. The Visitor Center
3. Contemporary Art Museum
4. Hess Collection Wine Shop
5. Self-guided iPod® Audio Tours
6. Tour of the Palate
7. The Garden
8. Auditorium
9. Hess Collection Wines
10. Wine Tasting and Tours

1 The Winery
The ivy-covered, three-story stone winery *(main image)* was erected in 1903 by wine merchant Colonel Theodore Gier. In 1930, it sold to the Christian Brothers religious order and was renovated by Donald Hess after he leased it from the order in 1989.

2 The Visitor Center
Housed in one of the original winery buildings, the visitor center features a wall of glass that offers a peek into the cool, dark Barrel Chai, a cellar where wine is aged in huge barrels.

3 Contemporary Art Museum
The private art collection of winery proprietor Donald Hess displays about 150 works, such as *Cornelia* by Anslem Kiefer *(above)*, and other names such as Frank Stella and Robert Motherwell, alongside other international artists.

Do not miss the porthole window in the Art Museum with a view down over the bottling line.

Hess Collection Wine Shop 4

The store *(right)* sells the Hess Collection labels of Mount Veeder appellation wines, Hess Select, and Hess Estate labels from appellations further afield. It also stocks small production wines from their small block series, only available at the winery.

Self-guided iPod® Audio Tours 5

There are no organized guided tours of the art collection, but you can pick up an iPod® and earphones at the visitor center and take a free self-guided walking tour at your own pace.

The Garden 7

The terraced winery garden is planted with native and exotic grasses and ornamentals, plus fern groves that edge up to redwood forest. Installations include various sculptures and a reflecting pool by noted landscape architect Peter Walker.

Auditorium 8

A 15-minute video presentation is given in this modern and comfy 40-seat theater. It gives an in-depth introduction to the winery, vineyards, and eco-sensitive, organic techniques, such as the use of goats for undergrowth management.

Tour of the Palate 6

This tour option, which is offered Thursday through Saturday, combines a guided tour of the art museum with a tasting of three release wines paired with dishes prepared by the winery's executive chef *(below)*.

Know Your AVAs

American Viticultural Areas (AVAs) are distinct geographical areas recognized for having unique conditions of terrain, soil, and climate distinct from their neighbors, resulting in characteristic wines. Although often referred to as appellations, the two terms are not synonymous. Appellations describe a generic geographic area rather than one defined by unique grape-growing characteristics. Thus an appellation can be an AVA, but not all are.

Hess Collection Wines 9

The winery's signature label wines are known for their complexity and elegance, exemplified by the flagship Mount Veeder Cabernet Sauvignon *(right)* and the Mount Veeder Chardonnay.

Wine Tasting and Tours 10

Options for sampling Hess wines include a private tasting of current releases, wine and cheese pairings, and tutorials by certified sommeliers. Themed winery tours are also offered by reservation and include tastings.

Left *Crowd I*, Magdalena Abakanowicz Right *Homage*, Leopoldo Maler

Artworks in The Hess Collection

Self-Portrait (2010)
Chinese artist Yue Minjun depicts himself cloned in mirthful multiple mirror images in this painting. His cynical guffaw is considered a commentary on contemporary China.

Self-Portrait, Yue Minjun

Elegy to the Spanish Republic (1979)
One in a series of canvases by Robert Motherwell (1915–91), a founding member of the American School of Abstract Expressionism, this painting has splattered black ovals and vertical bars against a white background.

Cornelia (2003)
German artist Anselm Kiefer's life-size depiction of a woman in a wedding gown with her upper body imprisoned in razor wire is a haunting reference to the Nazi period. The sculpture is housed in the garden, in a prison-like hut with rectangular viewing slits.

Johanna II (1985–86)
Swiss artist Franz Gertsch's hyper-realist painting, of a young woman gazing hypnotically at the viewer, is based on a projected slide. Pointillist technique (using small dots of pure color) has been used to achieve creative depth.

Staying in the Water (1987)
Carved from camphor wood, Japanese artist Katsura Funakoshi's poetic sculpture depicts a human figure from the waist up, dressed in a buttoned-up shirt with a cummerbund. The crown of the head is left unpainted and the grain of the wood serves as the hair.

Homage (1974)
Argentinian conceptual artist Leopoldo Maler's *Homage* is a paean to his uncle – an esteemed writer – who was assassinated for his inflammatory essays. The installation is an antique Underwood typewriter with a hidden gas burner.

Surface Tension (1991)
Created by famed British environmental "sculptor" Andy Goldsworthy, this work is an ad hoc lattice

Third Floor

Second Floor

First Floor

Key

	First floor
	Second Floor
	Third floor

The Hess Art Museum covers more than 13,000 sq ft (1,200 sq m) in a loft-like custom-made museum.

Donald Hess

Donald Hess was born in 1936 in Bern, Switzerland, into a brewing and hotelier family. He took over the family business at the age of 20 and refocused it as a bottled mineral water company. In 1978 he bought his first vineyard at Mount Veeder in Napa; today, Hess Family Estates own eight wineries on four continents. Hess began collecting art in 1966, when he bought a print that later proved to be an original Picasso. He has since amassed what Art in America magazine has called one of the world's top 200 private collections. Virtually all contemporary media are represented, from painting and sculpture to photography and installation, many of which are provocative mirrors of the cultural values of each artist's time. As a self-taught patron of the arts, Hess's purchases are driven by a passionate response to each piece – often he wakes up at night thinking about a work he has seen – and a personal rapport with the artist.

Donald Hess

Surface Tension, Andy Goldsworthy

created from chestnut leaf stalks held together with hawthorn needles, which also attach it to the walls, ceiling, and floor. *Surface Tension* reflects a passion for environmentalism that Donald Hess and Goldsworthy shared.

Tundra (1959)

8 This wild tricolor – red, green, and cream – by Greek-American painter Theodoros Stamos (1922–97) lets the viewers conjure their own conception of what the work depicts.

Crowd I (1986–87)

9 These 19 life-size, naked, and headless figures seem to advance from one corner of the room. Fashioned from resin and burlap by Polish sculptor Magdalena Abakanowicz, they reflect her experience growing up in communist Poland and symbolize the mindlessness of living in a totalitarian state.

Silverstone II (1982)

10 A three-dimensional image by American painter and printmaker Frank Stella, this mixed media piece uses aeronautical grade aluminum and automobile paint to depict the Silverstone racetrack in England.

Donald Hess buys the works of 20 living artists whose art he supports long term.

Napa Valley Wine Train

More than merely a restaurant on wheels, the Napa Valley Wine Train offers one of the most unique ways of seeing Wine Country, recalling the heyday of steam when Victorian-era travelers arrived to partake of the region's spas and early wineries. Diners eat aboard restored early 20th-century rail cars pulled by an antique locomotive that runs on 25 miles (40 km) of track parallel to Highway 29, through the heart of the valley. The relaxing 3-hour journey between the towns of Napa and St. Helena includes lunch or dinner, plus options for winery tours and special wine events.

View from Napa Valley Wine Train

After your tour, it is well worth traversing the same route along Hwy 29, taking time to stop at places that appealed as seen through the train windows.

Wine is not included in most lunch or dinner packages, so plan it as an added expense.

• Napa Valley Wine Train: 1275 McKinstry St., Napa, 94559; Map M5; 707 253 2111; Departures at 9:50am & 5:50pm; Reservations required: 800 427 4124; www.winetrain.com

Top 10 Features

1. Wine Education Dinner
2. Locomotives
3. Vista Dome
4. McKinstry Street Station
5. Murder Mystery Dinner Theater
6. Ambassador Winery Tour
7. Moonlight Escapes
8. "I do" Choo Choo
9. Pullman Rail Cars
10. A Movable Feast

1 Wine Education Dinner

These themed dinners aboard the Vista Dome car combine a culinary adventure with learning. Local wine experts, including celebrity wine makers, share their knowledge of viticulture during paired wine-and-food meals.

2 Locomotives

Built in Montreal, Canada, in 1958 and 1959, the two Wine Train locomotives originally hauled freight and had diesel engines, plus steam generators to heat the passenger cars. They have since been converted to operate on compressed natural gas, reducing emissions by more than three-quarters.

3 Vista Dome

A glass of sparkling wine welcomes guests in the elevated 1952 Pullman domed observation carriage, with huge windows that curve up to the ceiling. The bi-level car, which features a passenger compartment above and a kitchen below, first entered service in 1952 *(above).*

The original Napa Valley Railroad Company began train services in 1865 along a route that extended as far as Calistoga.

4 McKinstry Street Station
The railroad and squat square station were built in 1964 by California's first millionaire, Sam Brannan, to service his new spa hotel in Calistoga. Today the Napa Valley Wine Train Depot Station includes a wrap-around deck, wine shop, gift shop, lounge plus piano bar, and an informative visitor center *(above)*.

5 Murder Mystery Dinner Theater
Guests signing up for this monthly special event tour are offered a four-course dinner and four-act drama based on the illicit world of the gumshoe detective. Dress in period costume and help solve the mystery.

6 Ambassador Winery Tour
Combining on-board lunch with the journey, this tour option includes wine-tasting tuition plus visits by motorcoach to Raymond Vineyards winery and ZD Wines – an organic winery – for tours and tasting *(above)*.

7 Moonlight Escapes
Offered once a month to coincide with a full moon, this gourmet champagne dining package adds romance to the journey as silver moonlight washes over the vineyards of Napa Valley.

9 Pullman Rail Cars
The nine passenger carriages were built in 1915 by the Pullman Company and have been revamped with mahogany paneling, brass accents, etched glass partitions, and velvet-covered armchairs *(above)*.

8 "I do" Choo Choo
Many guests choose the Wine Train as a venue to propose marriage, celebrate an anniversary, renew their wedding vows, or even wed. The company's special events department offers wedding and similar packages, including an elopement plan.

10 A Movable Feast
The Wine Train offers lunch and dinner options in either the Pullman cars or the Vista Dome. Each has its own distinct ambience and menu, with fine china and flowers.

Judgment of Paris
In 1976, British wine merchant Steven Spurrier organized a blind tasting in France, where wines grown in Bordeaux and Burgundy were pitted against the wines from California. The French judges gave top honours to Stag's Leap Wine Cellars Cabernet and Chateau Montelena Chardonnay, resulting in a newfound recognition of California wines worldwide.

If you book a mid-winter dinner package, you'll be traveling in the dark and won't see the valley.

⭕10 Calistoga

Located at the northern end of Napa Valley, this resort town was laid out as a spa destination in the 1860s by millionaire businessman Sam Brannan as a West Coast equivalent to Saratoga Springs in New York. While drunk, Brannan proclaimed that it would be the "Calistoga of Sarafornia!" The slow-paced town sits atop thermal springs that supply its many spas. The main street and leafy backstreets are lined with historic stone, brick, and timber buildings housing eclectic stores, inns, and restaurants. Wineries and several natural attractions within walking distance add to Calistoga's charm.

Dr. Wilkinson's Hot Springs Resort

🔵 Start your day with granola with fruit and yogurt at the Calistoga Roastery (1426 Lincoln Av., Calistoga, 94515).

• Calistoga Visitor Center: 1133 Washington St., Calistoga, 94515; Map K2; www.calistogavisitors.com
• Old Faithful Geyser of California: 1299 Tubbs Ln.; Map K2; www.oldfaithfulgeyser.com
• Dr Wilkinson's Hot Springs Resort: 1507 Lincoln Av.; Map K2; www.drwilkinson.com
• Clos Pegase Winery: 1060 Dunaweal Ln.; Map K3; www.clospegase.com • Calistoga Pioneer Cemetery: Foothill Blvd.; Map K2 • Calistoga Depot: 1458 Lincoln Av.; Map K2 • www.calistogaballoons.com
• Schramsberg Vineyards: 1400 Schramsberg Rd.; Map K3; www.schramsberg.com • Sterling Vineyards: 1111 Dunaweal Ln.; Map K2; www.sterling vineyards.com • Castello di Amorosa: 4045 N. St. Helena Hwy.; Map K3; www.castellodi amorosa.com

Top 10 Features

1. Lincoln Avenue
2. Old Faithful Geyser of California
3. Dr. Wilkinson's Hot Springs Resort
4. Clos Pegase Winery
5. Calistoga Pioneer Cemetery
6. Calistoga Depot
7. Calistoga Balloons
8. Schramsberg Vineyards
9. Sterling Vineyards
10. Castello di Amorosa

Lincoln Avenue
Calistoga's tree-lined main street *(above)* invites leisurely exploration on foot to admire its vintage storefronts, browse bookshops and art galleries, sample wines, and perhaps enjoy an impromptu spa treatment.

Old Faithful Geyser of California
One of only three geysers in the world that erupt at regular intervals, Old Faithful shoots a jet of scalding water 100 ft (35 m) in the air every 30 minutes *(right)*.

Dr. Wilkinson's Hot Springs Resort
This heart-of-town spa, founded in 1952 by Dr. John Wilkinson, is famous for its signature therapeutic mud bath in which guests float in a mixture of volcanic ash, hot mineral water, and peat.

Calistoga was named an official Napa Valley AVA (American Viticultural Area) in December 2009.

Clos Pegase Winery
Named for the mythical horse, Pegasus, this winery *(above)* has 20th-century works of art displayed in its sculpture garden. Its modern architecture by Michael Graves is also a highlight. Barrel-aging caves extend into a rocky knoll that rises from the vineyards.

Calistoga Pioneer Cemetery
Remains of Napa Valley pioneers and Civil War veterans lie beneath tombstones shaded by oaks. Look for the grave of Bud Philpot, a stagecoach driver killed in a 1881 hold-up.

Calistoga Depot
Listed as a National Historic Building, Calistoga Depot was built in 1888. The depot and six antique railroad carriages house a wine center, and railroad memorabilia *(above)*.

Calistoga Balloons
Float over wineries in a hot-air balloon, experiencing the valley from a new angle. Trips begin around dawn.

Schramsberg Vineyards
An obligatory guided tour of this winery, founded in 1867, includes founder Jacob Schram's Victorian mansion, plus barrel-aging caves. Visitors can learn how sparkling wines are made, and opt for a tasting experience.

Sterling Vineyards
Perched atop a rocky knoll, Sterling Vineyards is reached by an aerial tram. The brilliant white architecture mimics that of the Greek island of Mýkonos. The self-guided winery tour is enhanced by motion-activated information screens.

Castello di Amorosa
Replicating a medieval Italian castle *(right)*, this winery offers horse-drawn carriage tours through the vineyards, past historic relics, such as Napa Valley's first schoolhouse.

Steep in Mud

Calistoga's signature spa treatment is a hot mud bath. Participants float, as if weightless, while cocooned in a mixture of warm, soft volcanic ash from nearby Mount Konocti, peat, and mineral water scented with lavender. The treatment is said to improve skin complexion, remove toxins, and relieve joint and muscle pain.

Wappo American Indians originally combined volcanic ash with warm spring water to make a mud bath.

🔟 Culinary Institute of America

Listed on the National Register of Historic Places since 1978, the castle-like Greystone Cellars rises majestically over Highway 29 immediately north of St. Helena. Once the Wine Country's largest winery, today it is a branch of the New York-based Culinary Institute of America (CIA) serving as a teaching campus for the culinary arts and offering courses for professionals, plus cooking and wine-appreciation demonstrations for visitors. Added draws for the public are a herb garden, vineyards, educational theaters, plus a café and restaurant, making a visit here a rounded educational experience about food and wine.

Façade, Culinary Institute of America

🕙 The CIA Greystone Cellars website includes an online tour of the campus.

🍽 Dine at the Wine Spectator Greystone Restaurant and watch chefs working at open cooking stations. The Bakery Café by illy sells breads, pastries, and other baked goods produced by the institute's students, as well as coffee and tea.

• Map L3; 2555 Main St., St. Helena, 94574; 800 888 7850; Cooking Demonstrations and Courses Reservations: 707 967 1010; Flavor Bar: Open 10am–6pm daily; www.ciachef.edu/california, www.ciastore.com

Top 10 Features

1. Greystone Cellars
2. Student Garden
3. Cannard Herb Garden
4. Spice Islands Marketplace
5. Brother Timothy's Corkscrew Collection
6. Flavor Bar
7. Food and Wine Museum
8. Cooking Demonstrations and Courses
9. Vintners Hall of Fame
10. The Ecolab Theatre

Greystone Cellars
Built in 1889 of native tufa stone in Richardsonian-Romanesque fashion, this three-story edifice features grand arches and cathedral ceilings *(main image)*. Greystone's original oak front doors open to an atrium that soars 90 ft (30 m).

Student Garden
The Sutter Home Organic Garden, also known as the Student Garden, supplies much of the fresh produce for the institute's kitchens. The garden is open to workshop participants. In-garden lectures provide insights into sustainable agriculture.

Cannard Herb Garden
Located in front and to the left of the Greystone Cellars building, this small terraced garden *(left)* grows more than 60 species of culinary herbs and 11 species of berries. Salad greens, onions, herbal tea, apples, and edible flowers are also grown.

Spice Islands Marketplace
A wish-list of culinary-related items are sold in this store (above), from cookware and cutlery to CIA culinary class DVDs, local specialty ingredients, wine accessories, and more than 1,700 cookbooks – many autographed by the author.

Flavor Bar
Here, visitors enjoy a "Taste Like a Chef" sensory experience that gives insights into how chefs decide what ingredients to use (below). The Oleoteca introduces them to the production, tasting, and use of "super-premium" olive oils made from olives harvested at the peak of freshness and flavor.

Vintners Hall of Fame
With its beamed ceilings and historic 2,200-gallon wine barrels, the Vintners Hall of Fame celebrates individuals who have contributed to California's wine industry, marked by sculpted bronze plaques.

The Ecolab Theatre
Rising two levels, the 125-seat amphitheater-style Ecolab Theatre is designed for cooking demonstrations, lectures, and tastings. Tiered seating and video monitors offer grandstand views of the 22 ft (7 m) cooking center (left).

Brother Timothy's Corkscrew Collection
More than 1,800 corkscrews from around the world were amassed over several decades by Brother Timothy, Christian Brothers' winemaker, who began his collection in 1949 (below).

Food and Wine Museum
Illustrating the history of Greystone Cellars, this exhibit includes an ancient stone olive press, a copper still, and miscellaneous winemaking artifacts.

Cooking Demonstrations and Courses
The De Baun Theatre hosts cooking demonstrations, and amateur chefs can choose weekend courses or 2- to 5-day "Boot Camp" courses offered in the top floor teaching kitchens.

The Christian Brothers

This worldwide Catholic order has played an important part in the history of Napa Valley viticulture. In 1950, the Christian Brothers bought Greystone to produce brandy and sparkling wine. Their wine-chemist, Anthony George Diener, "Brother Timothy" (1910–2004), was a pioneer in the California wine industry. The order sold Greystone in 1989.

The Culinary Institute of America still makes wines under the Greystone label, from grapes grown on a small vineyard nearby.

TOP 10 The Silverado Trail

Running along the eastern side of Napa Valley beneath the oak-studded peaks of the Vaca Mountains, this historic highway – named for the Silverado Silver Mine – connects the towns of Napa and Calistoga. It is more serene than Highway 29, which runs through the center of the valley and can be thronged with traffic on weekends. Rolling, gently winding in sections, and elevated over the valley, the Silverado Trail is popular for cycling. Many small mom-and-pop wineries line the route, alongside some big-name wineries such as Darioush and Stag's Leap.

Wine samples, Darioush

🌿 Visitors with deep pockets should book the Quintessential Wine Experience at Darioush.

• Silverado Resort and Spa: 1600 Atlas Peak Rd., Napa, 94558; Map M4; www.silverado resort.com • Soda Canyon Store: 4006 Silverado Trail, Napa, 94558 • Darioush: 4240 Silverado Trail, Napa, 94558 • Omi Farm: 4185 Silverado Trail, Napa, 94558; Map M4 • Clos du Val: 5330 Silverado Trail, Napa, 94558; Map M4 • Stag's Leap Winery: 6150 Silverado Trail, Napa, 94558; Map M4 • Cliff Lede Winery: 1473 Yountville Crossroad, Yountville, 94599; Map L4 • Napa River Ecological Reserve: Yountville Crossroad, Yountville; Map L4 • Joseph Phelps Vineyards: 200 Taplin Rd., St. Helena, 94574; Map L3 • Casa Nuestra Winery: 3451 Silverado Trail N., St. Helena, 94574; Map L3

Top 10 Features

1. Silverado Resort and Spa
2. Soda Canyon Store
3. Darioush
4. Omi Farm
5. Clos du Val
6. Stag's Leap Winery
7. Cliff Lede Winery
8. Napa River Ecological Reserve
9. Joseph Phelps Vineyards
10. Casa Nuestra Winery

1 Silverado Resort and Spa

With 435 deluxe suites, the Silverado Resort and Spa *(above)* boasts the largest resort spa in Napa Valley, plus two golf courses, 13 tennis courts, and 10 outdoor swimming pools.

2 Soda Canyon Store

A well-stocked grocery and delicatessen, this store, about 2 miles (3 km) north of Napa, is a great place to stock up on picnic items, which can be enjoyed in picnic grounds or on a shaded patio overlooking a creek and vineyard.

4 Omi Farm

Although this family-run farm has a small vineyard producing Cabernet Sauvignon grapes for local wineries, owners Kirsten and Jim Niesar also grow fruits, nuts, and vegetables, and raise chickens, guinea hens, rabbits, sheep, and even Australian Cattle Dogs *(above)*.

3 Darioush

The freestanding columns, fountains, and lush gardens at Darioush evoke the ancient Persian capital of Persepolis, reflecting the owner's heritage *(main image)*.

Originating as an ancient Wappo Indian path, in 1852 the trail became a wagon route to and from the Silverado Silver Mine.

Clos du Val
Renowned for its award-winning wines, Clos du Val's other draws include beautiful grounds, *pétanque* courts, and a winery that hosts casual tastings and formal tours *(above)*.

Stag's Leap Winery
This winery leapt to prominence in 1976 when its Cabernet Sauvignon won the Judgment of Paris. It has lovely gardens, a barrel cave lit by sconces, and 17th-century original paintings of ancient celestial maps.

Cliff Lede Winery
This Stag's Leap AVA winery features a sophisticated cave storage system, and a welcoming tasting room. The highlight is a contemporary art gallery housed in a former fermentation room.

Olive Oils
Though vineyards dominate the landscape of Wine Country, the warm Mediterranean climate of the Napa and Sonoma Valleys is also ideal for growing olives, which were first planted here by Franciscan missionaries in the mid-1700s. There are now more than 150 local producers, and the pressing of gourmet, artisanal extra virgin olive oil is big business. California's olive oils range from buttery yellow to light green, and are typically more robust than those of Italy or Spain. Many boutique producers have tasting rooms.

Napa River Ecological Reserve
In dry months, a single trail of the Napa river winds through this floodplain wilderness. It irrigates meadows, shrub thickets, and stands of oak and willow that provide shelter and food for wildlife.

Joseph Phelps Vineyards
Perched on a hilltop, this winery offers lovely views over the valley. Its award-winning Insignia Bordeaux-blend and other red wines can be enjoyed on the tasting terrace *(above)*.

Casa Nuestra Winery
Casa Nuestra's wine labels display a dove, "Ban the Bomb" sign, and the words "Embrace Peace." The tasting room exhibits clippings about Mother Teresa and Nelson Mandela, plus Elvis Presley memorabilia.

The Silverado Trail Wineries Association's website (www.silveradotrail.com) has links to more than 40 member wineries.

🔟 Sonoma State Historic Park

Centered on Sonoma's old central plaza, Sonoma State Historic Park enshrines about one dozen mostly Spanish and Mexican buildings dating back to 1823. The square – the largest of its kind in California – and its surrounding grid of streets were laid out by Mexican General Mariano Vallejo in 1836, around the site of California's northernmost Franciscan mission. Vallejo's own home, Lachryma Montis, is a 10-minute walk from the plaza, but houses the visitor center and is a centerpiece of the 36-acre (15-ha) park, site of the 1846 Bear Flag Revolt that led to California officially becoming a U.S. state.

Sonoma Cheese Factory

🅾 **Sonoma Cheese Factory (2 Spain St., 800 535 2855) sells salads, sandwiches, and a variety of cheese.**

- Map L5
- Visitors Bureau: 363 3rd St. W., Sonoma 95476; www.parks. ca.gov • City Hall: 1 The Plaza • Toscano Hotel: Sonoma Plaza, Spain St. between 2nd & 4th; http://sonoma league. org/toscano.html
- Lachryma Montis: 363 3rd St. W. • General Joseph Hooker House: 414 1st St. E.; http:// sonomaleague.org/ vasquez.html • Somona Barracks: E. Spain St. & 1st St. E. • Mission San Francisco Solano di Sonoma: E. Spain St. & 1st St. E. • Bear Flag Monument: E. Spain St. & 1st St. E., Sonoma Plaza • Blue Wing Inn: 133 E. Spain St.; www. bluewingadobe.org • La Casa Grande Servants' Quarters: E. Spain St. between 1st St. W. and 1st St. E., Sonoma Plaza

Top 10 Features

1. Sonoma Plaza
2. City Hall
3. Toscano Hotel
4. Lachryma Montis
5. General Joseph Hooker House
6. Sonoma Barracks
7. Mission San Francisco Solano
8. Bear Flag Monument
9. Blue Wing Inn
10. La Casa Grande Servants' Quarters

1 Sonoma Plaza
This graceful, grassy plaza is the town's focal point and has walkways radiating out in six directions from City Hall, at its heart. It is lined with historic buildings, shops and restaurants.

3 Toscano Hotel
On the north side of the plaza, the Toscano Hotel is maintained as it looked a century ago, with period furnishings and antique photos *(right)*. A downstairs dining room is laid out as if guests will appear at any minute and includes a board announcing the day's menu.

2 City Hall
Occupying the center of the plaza, the City Hall *(left)* was built in 1908 with identical façades on four sides. It serves as city council headquarters.

Lachryma Montis
In 1850, General Vallejo purchased a land tract northwest of the plaza and built a Gothic-style Victorian home beside a spring that the Indian's called Chiucuyem (tears of the mountain). Vallejo translated it into Latin, hence the name *(above)*.

Mission San Francisco Solano
The mission building and its adobe chapel *(main image)* date from 1832. It displays exhibits of mission life. A monument on its west side honors 896 American Indians buried there.

Blue Wing Inn
Once an army barracks, this inn was later expanded to become a hotel that welcomed guests such as Ulysses S. Grant and Kit Carson.

Bear Flag Monument
This monument marks the rebellion on June 14, 1846, when a group of U.S. settlers arrested General Vallejo and declared the inception of the Republic of California *(left)*.

La Casa Grande Servants' Quarters
General Vallejo's first home, La Casa Grande was built in 1840 but destroyed by fire in 1867. This building is all that remains. A good example of adobe construction.

General Joseph Hooker House
Relocated to its present site in 2008 and formerly known as the "Vasquéz House," the restored simple clapboard home of Civil War General "Fighting Joe" Hooker now serves as a museum of Sonoma history.

Sonoma Barracks
Completed in 1841 to house General Vallejo's Mexican troops, the Sonoma Barracks were taken over by U.S. Dragoons in 1849 and later served as a winery *(above)*.

American Indian Servitude
When Spanish missionaries established their 21 California missions (1769–1833), they attempted to convert the American Indians to Christianity and teach them skills useful to the Spanish empire. They enslaved the Indians, who worked under brutal regimentation. Many "Mission Indians" rebelled and destroyed mission buildings. The program ended in 1834.

Visitors can park for free in the large parking lot behind the Toscano Hotel and Sonoma Barracks.

Left **Ornamental trim** Center **The Chalet** Right **Napoleon's Cottage**

🔝10 Features of Lachryma Montis

1 Gothic Architecture

General Mariano Vallejo's two-story wooden home, which was prefabricated in New England and shipped around Cape Horn to California, is a perfect example of Victorian-era Carpenter Gothic architecture. Pointed arches, steep gables, and a large Gothic window in the master bedroom are the house's dominant features. The interior is brick-lined for insulation against heat and cold.

2 Ornamental Trim

The house's eaves are decorated with elaborately carved wooden trim called "gingerbread." The jigsaw details were made possible by the invention of the steam-powered scroll saw in the mid-1800s.

3 The Chalet

Prefabricated to originally serve as the home's warehouse, this stone-and-timber building was converted to a small guest house – the "Swiss Chalet." Today it serves as the park's visitor center and museum, with exhibits on the life of General Vallejo and Lachryma Montis.

4 El Delirio

This simple yet delightful garden pavilion with a name suggesting ecstasy is west of the main house and was used

Lachryma Montis

as a guest cottage. Vallejo wrote his *La História de California* (History of California) here.

5 Swan Fountain

Standing in front of El Delirio, this decorative fountain is perched atop a basin and wrought-iron pedestal decorated with long curling leaves. The namesake swan has its wings spread apart, while its long outstretched neck and bill spout water.

Swan Fountain

6 Fruit Trees

General Vallejo planted many species of fruit trees, including apples, apricots, peaches, plums, and citrus, as well as grapevines transplanted from La Casa Grande, his

Vallejo's notes and first draft of his La História de California *were destroyed in the Casa Grande fire in 1867.*

General Vallejo

Born in Monterey, California, on July 7, 1808, Mariano Guadelupe Vallejo rose to become an outstanding native Californian of his day. He initiated a career in the Mexican army and led many campaigns against American Indians. In 1833 he

General Vallejo

was named commander of the Presidio of San Francisco, and later that year founded Sonoma. He briefly served as governor of Alta California, was a member of the first Constitutional Convention of California after the Bear Flag Revolt, accepted annexation of California by the United States, and was elected to the State Senate. Vallejo lived at Lachryma Montis for 35 years, but was gradually dispossessed of most of his property and lived his later years in relative poverty. He also wrote a five-volume History of California (La História de California) before his death in 1890. The city of Vallejo, which he founded, is named after him.

first home in Sonoma. Decorative trees and shrubs also grace the garden.

Napoleon's Cottage
Officially called "The Hermitage," this tiny cabin was built for Vallejo's son, Napoleon. As a youth, Napoleon lived with a menagerie that included 14 dogs. It is reached by a stone staircase behind the reservoir.

Driveway
Stretching for more than a quarter mile (400 m), the driveway was lined with cottonwood trees and rose bushes. Many old trees still stand alongside newly planted ones. Expansive meadows spread out to each side.

Personal Effects
Lachryma Montis is furnished with period pieces, including many of Vallejo's personal

effects. The dining room is laid out as if guests are expected for dinner. Note the white-marble fireplace and the French rosewood piano in the living room.

Freshwater Reservoir
Surrounded by a vine-covered arbor, this stone-and-brick reservoir was built by Vallejo to capture water from the natural springs. The arbor provides shade for ducks and turtles that paddle around in the water.

Freshwater Reservoir

Santa Rosa

By far the largest city in Wine Country, Santa Rosa is the gateway to the Russian River. While many visitors pass through without stopping, the city is replete with attractions, including superb museums ranging from bastions of high culture, such as the Sonoma County Museum, to the Charles M. Schulz Museum, honoring the cartoonist and his creation, Snoopy. The city's downtown core, anchored by Railroad Square, has been revitalized as a lively center for arts, fine dining, and entertainment. Santa Rosa is also a great base for outdoor activities in the surrounding hills.

Restaurant, Railroad Square Historic District

Petite Syrah is a local gourmet specialty restaurant in the Railroad Square Historic District *(see p59).*

Top 10 Features

1. Luther Burbank Home & Gardens
2. Charles M. Schulz Museum
3. Sonoma County Museum
4. The Civic Artwalk
5. Shiloh Ranch Regional Park
6. Railroad Square Historic District
7. Prince Memorial Greenway
8. Church of One Tree
9. Kendall-Jackson Wine Center & Gardens
10. Safari West

• www.visitsantarosa.com • Luther Burbank Home & Gardens: 204 Santa Rosa Av., 95404; Map Q3; www.lutherburbank.org • Charles M. Schulz Museum: 2301 Hardies Ln., 95403; Map J3; www.schulzmuseum.org • Sonoma County Museum: 425 7th St., 95401; Map N1; www.sonomacountymuseum.org • Shiloh Ranch Regional Park: 5750 Faught Rd.; Map J3 • Railroad Square Historic District: Davis St., between 3rd & 6th, 95401; Map N2; http://railroadsquare.net • Church of One Tree: 492 Sonoma Av., 95401; Map P3 • Kendall-Jackson Wine Center: 5007 Fulton Rd., Fulton, 95439; Map J3; www.kj.com/visit/wine-center • www.safariwest.com

Luther Burbank Home & Gardens
Horticulturist Luther Burbank (1849–1926) lived in this Greek Revival house and conducted plant-breeding experiments in its gardens. The home, furnished as it was on the day of his death, has a museum *(above).*

Charles M. Schulz Museum
Dedicated to cartoonist Charles M. Schulz, this museum houses exhibits such as Schulz's studio with original art that traces the evolution of Charlie Brown and his pet dog Snoopy *(main image).*

Sonoma County Museum
This museum occupies the historic Post Office building, built in 1909 in Roman Renaissance Revival style. Its rotating exhibits – from paintings and sculptures to home décor – interpret the art, culture, and history of Wine Country *(right).*

Mountain lions are occasionally spotted roaming Santa Rosa's outskirts.

The Civic Artwalk

Downtown Santa Rosa is dotted with sculptures to beautify the city. The Artwalk begins with Stan Pawlowski's *Peanuts* statue *(right)* at Depot Park in Railroad Square, and includes 37 other public artworks.

Shiloh Ranch Regional Park

This 850-acre (344-ha) park in the hills northeast of Santa Rosa provides a bucolic escape from city life. Mules, deer, gray foxes, and coyotes are seen on trails that snake through the woodlands.

Railroad Square Historic District

Built by Italian stonemasons at the turn of the 20th century, the buildings in this district today serve as restaurants, specialty shops, and bars *(below)*.

MUSEUM AND RESEARCH CENTER

Prince Memorial Greenway

This lush half-a-mile (one-km) long corridor links Santa Rosa's Railroad Square to City Hall. Historic buildings, murals, and sculptures flank the creek.

Church of One Tree

Built in 1873 from the wood of a single redwood tree, this church *(left)* houses the Robert L. Ripley Memorial Museum. It is a tribute to anthropologist Robert LeRoy Ripley (1890–1949), who created the Ripley's Believe It or Not! franchise.

Kendall-Jackson Wine Center & Gardens

This cavernous winery in French-chateau style is set amid 120 acres (49 ha) of gardens and vines. The gardens are a delight in any season and include themed parterres. The winery offers wine tastings from the Kendall-Jackson empire, including Australia.

Safari West

Home to many exotic birds and mammals, this wildlife preserve is explored in open-air safari vehicles. Giraffe, gazelles, ostrich, and zebra are among the African animals that roam the park.

Charles M. Schulz

Cartoonist Charles M. Schulz was born in Minneapolis on November 26, 1922, and spent much of his youth reading comics. He had his first cartoon published in 1937. Schulz served as a machine-gunner in WW II, and, in 1950, debuted "Peanuts," the comic strip that launched him to fame and made Snoopy, the cartoon dog, a world-recognized figure. Schulz settled in Santa Rosa in 1969 and died here in 2000.

Author, celebrity chef, TV personality, and cooking show host Guy Fieri lives in Santa Rosa and owns five restaurants in the area.

🔟 Russian River

The sprawling Russian River region straddles the namesake river that carves through the coastal mountain range. This area of rolling hills and majestic redwood forests is unsurpassed for outdoor activities, from kayaking and canoeing to fishing and hiking. Riverside towns such as Guerneville retain their early frontier spirit, while the Victorian town of Healdsburg has emerged as a trendy center of wine-tasting rooms, fine restaurants, and boutique hotels, and is the perfect base for exploring the region. Wines made here rival those of neighboring AVAs, and the region is also a center for hop production.

Armstrong Redwoods Natural Reserve

🌐 An organic grocery store, Food for Humans (First St. & Mill St., Guerneville; 707 869 3612), sells cheese and produce.

• www.russianriver.com
• HKG Estate Wines: 6050 Westside Rd., Healdsburg, 95448; Map H3; www.hkgwines.com
• Korbel Champagne Cellars: 13250 River Rd., Guerneville, 95446; Map H3; www.korbel.com
• Rodney Strong Vineyards: 11455 Old Redwood Hwy., Healdsburg, 95448; Map H2; www.rodneystrong.com • www.healdsburg.com • Canoeing: www.burkescanoetrips.com
• Foppiano Vineyards: 12707 Old Redwood Hwy., Healdsburg, 95448; Map H2; www.foppiano.com • Russian River Jazz and Blues Festival: www.russianriverfestivals.com • Armstrong Redwoods State Natural Reserve: 17000 Armstrong Woods Rd., Guerneville, 95446; Map G3; www.parks.ca.gov

Top 10 Features

1. HKG Estate Wines
2. River Road
3. Korbel Champagne Cellars
4. Guerneville
5. Rodney Strong Vineyards
6. Healdsburg
7. Canoeing
8. Foppiano Vineyards
9. Russian River Jazz and Blues Festival
10. Armstrong Redwoods State Natural Reserve

1 HKG Estate Wines

Dominated by a towering old hop kiln *(above)* that today serves as a tasting room, this winery is known for its full-bodied red wines and proprietary blends of Chardonnay, Pinot Noir, and Pinot Grigio.

3 Korbel Champagne Cellars

Renowned for its California Champagnes, Korbel *(right)* was founded in 1882 by three Czechoslovakian brothers. Its impressive stone-and-timber winery produces 1.7 million cases a year. The magnificent rose garden in front of the Korbel family house was planted more than a century ago.

2 River Road

Running alongside the lower Russian River, this winding and scenic two-lane road connects wide-open vineyards and riverside villages shaded by stands of ancient oaks and redwood trees. Midweek is the best time for a drive, when traffic is light.

Guerneville

This riverside town *(above)* is the heart of the Russian River resort area and is thronged on summer weekends, when Johnson's Beach is a popular venue for sunbathing and swimming. The historic Guerneville bridge spans the river.

Rodney Strong Vineyards

This signature winery has pioneered many innovations in the local wine industry. It offers complimentary tasting, guided tours, and hosts seasonal concerts.

Healdsburg

Located at the junction of the Alexander Valley, Dry Creek, and Russian River Valley AVAs, this charming town is replete with wine-tasting rooms, centered on a historic plaza *(below)*.

Foppiano Vineyards

Italian immigrant Giovanni Foppiano founded this winery in 1896. It produces four varietals, served in a cozy tasting room adjoining a century-old railroad caboose *(above)*.

Armstrong Redwoods State Natural Reserve

This wilderness protects 805 acres (326 ha) of stately California redwoods, the tallest trees on earth. Trails lead from a visitor center into an awe-inspiring grove.

Canoeing

Canoeing is a popular activity April through October when the river is slow-moving *(main image)*. Look out for herons, ospreys, and turtles.

Russian River Jazz and Blues Festival

Founded in 1976, this festival has evolved into one of the world's top jazz events. Hosted on Johnson's Beach, it draws leading jazz musicians.

Prohibition

The evangelical Protestant churches' campaign for a ban on the sale of alcohol resulted in the 1919 enactment of the Volstead Act. Wholesale prohibition was levied on the manufacture, sale, and transportation of wine, beer, and liquors, which decimated the California wine industry. The Prohibition amendment was revoked in 1933 but it took decades for the wine industry to recover.

Public-access beaches along the Russian River are perfect places to fish for bass, bluegill and salmon.

10 Alexander Valley

This long, narrow valley drained by the upper Russian River stretches 20 miles (32 km) north from Healdsburg to the agricultural town of Cloverdale via somnolent Geyserville, a center for geothermal energy. Although fogs seep in from the Russian River valley, the region's rich alluvial soils and high summer temperatures produce opulent wines. Separated by pastures and apple orchards, wineries here are less crowded than in the Napa and Sonoma valleys. A preponderance of Italian names reflects the immigrants who settled here in the late 19th century.

Boutique winery, Geyserville

Locals Tasting Room (Geyserville Av. & SR 128; 707 857 4900; Open daily 11am–6pm), in Geyserville, serves wines from 11 boutique wineries.

• Jimtown Store: 6706 Hwy. 128, Healdsburg, 95448; Map H2; 707 433 1212; www. jimtown.com • Stryker Sonoma: 5110 Hwy. 128, Geyserville, 95441; Map H1; 800 433 1944; www.strykersonoma. com • Clos du Bois Winery: 19410 Geyserville Av., Geyserville 95441; Map H1; www.closdubois. com • Geyserville Chamber of Commerce: Map H1; www. geyservillecc.com • Milt Brandt Visitor Center, Lake Sonoma: 707 431 4533 • Souverain: 26150 Asti Rd., Cloverdale, 95425; Map G1; www. souverain.com • Cloverdale Visitor Center: 124 N Cloverdale Blvd.; Map G1; www. cloverdale.net

Top 10 Features

1. Jimtown Store
2. Stryker Sonoma Winery
3. Francis Ford Coppola Winery
4. Clos du Bois Winery
5. Geyserville
6. Dry Creek Road
7. Lake Sonoma
8. Asti
9. Souverain
10. Cloverdale

Jimtown Store

This quaint deli-grocery in the midst of vineyards is the perfect spot to buy picnic goods or a delcious gourmet boxed lunch, or gift boxes of local items.

Stryker Sonoma Winery

The magnificent glass-walled tasting room here overlooks the vineyards *(above)* and westward over the Alexander Valley. Its Zinfandels from old vine grapes planted in the 1920s are a highlight.

Francis Ford Coppola Winery

Intended to be fun and family friendly, this winery *(right)* belongs to the famous Hollywood director *(see pp30–31)*.

Clos du Bois Winery

A friendly winery whose name means "enclosure in the woods," Clos du Bois features an airy tasting room plus land-scaped grounds perfect for picnics. Take the optional "Marlstone Experience" tour to visit the vineyards.

US 101 runs down the center of the valley, but most wineries line SR 128 south of Geyserville.

5 Geyserville
Straddling SR 128, this lovely town *(above)* boasts many grand Victorian mansions, plus false-front western buildings that line the main street. It is named for the many geysers that a century ago drew visitors, and have since been tapped for geothermal energy.

6 Dry Creek Road
This road runs through the compact, crowd-free Dry Creek Valley, which extends north from Healdsburg and is lined with tiny, family-run wineries. The region also has many plum and pear orchards.

7 Lake Sonoma
Created in 1883, this lake is popular for boating, swimming, bass fishing, and trails good for hiking and mountain biking.

8 Asti
Named for the town of Asti, in Piedmont, Italy, this community began life in the 1880s as a grape-growing cooperative, founded by Italian immigrant Andrea Sbarboro. It became the largest producer of table wine in California.

9 Souverain
Occupying the original Asti winery, Souverain is known for award-winning wines, including several reserve labels available only here. A tour takes in the original buildings, a huge barrel room, and Andrea Sbarboro's riverside villa *(above)*.

10 Cloverdale
This small, idyllic town at the north end of Alexander Valley invites leisurely strolling to admire and appreciate its Gothic and gingerbread Victorian homes. Highlights include the Cloverdale Historical Museum.

The Wappo
The Wappo tribe of American Indians occupied the Napa, Sonoma, and Alexander Valleys and Russian River region on the eve of Mexican colonization. Their name is a derivation of the Spanish word *guapo*, meaning handsome. There were approximately 8,000 Wappo still alive in 1850. Today the tribe is reduced to about 340 living members in the Alexander Valley.

The Alexander Valley is named for Cyrus Alexander, owner of the Rancho Sotoyome Mexican land grant of 1847.

📖 Francis Ford Coppola Winery

Appealing mainly to families and curiosity-seekers, this popular venue is the Disneyland of Wine Country wineries. It is also one of the most diverse, interesting, and unpretentious. Hollywood producer Francis Ford Coppola bought the French-style Chateau Souverain property in late 2005 and turned it into a family-focused resort winery offering fine dining, entertainment, and day-long relaxation in a festive atmosphere. A reflection of Coppola's typically Italian passion for wine, food, fun, and family, a visit here is richly rewarded, not least for a chance to see his Oscars plus iconic props from his movies.

Pool Café

🍽 The Pool Café, at the swimming pool, serves hot dogs and burgers, plus sandwiches, salads, and ice creams.

• Francis Ford Coppola Winery: 300 Via Archimedes, Geyserville, 95441; Map H2; 707 857 1400; Open 11am–9pm; Bottling Ballet Mechanique Tours: 11:30am, 1pm, 2:30pm & 4pm, $20 including wine-tasting; www.franciscoppolawinery.com

Top 10 Features

1. The Chateau
2. Movie Memorabilia
3. Rustic Bar
4. Performing Arts Pavilion
5. Bottling Ballet Mechanique
6. Bocce Ball Courts
7. RUSTIC
8. Movie Screens
9. Swimming Pool
10. The Labels

The Chateau

The grand, European-style stone winery has twin, hop kiln-like towers with sharply angled slate roofs. It is entered via a guest services building adorned with a large mural from Coppola's 1988 film *Tucker: the Man and His Dream*.

Movie Memorabilia

Various memorabilia from Coppola's movies are displayed on two levels. Icons include Colonel Kurtz's uniform *(Apocalypse Now)*, Corleone's desk *(The Godfather)*, and a rare 1948 Tucker automobile *(main image)* from *Tucker: The Man and His Dream*. Coppola's Oscars and Golden Globes are displayed in glass cases.

Rustic Bar

The Rustic Bar, outside the restaurant of the same name, serves a full menu of beer and cocktails. Movie memorabilia displayed here include the giant martini glass from *One from the Heart (above)* plus costumes from Bram Stoker's *Dracula*.

The winery produces more than 40 wines, which can be sampled on a variety of tasting tours.

Performing Arts Pavilion

This small neoclassical pavilion *(above)* beside the swimming pool patio is painted with murals and has amphitheater seating with vineyard views. It is a venue for free live entertainment every weekend from April through October, and for other special events.

Movie Screens

Flat-screen TVs affixed to walls throughout the movie galleries and bar show scenes from Coppola's movies themed to nearby displays, including *The Godfather, Apocalypse Now, Into the Heart of Darkness,* and *Marie Antoinette* by Coppola's daughter, Sofia.

Swimming Pool

The massive H-shaped, heated swimming pool is surrounded by sundecks with showers. Pool passes include towels and use of lounge chairs, and you can rent one of 28 cabins. Lifeguards are on duty at all times.

The Labels

The winery makes nearly four dozen wines known, not least, for their unusual labels, such as the Director's Cut line's spiral labels and the gold-colored netting of the Diamond Collection Pavilion and Claret *(left)*.

Bottling Ballet Mechanique

This 45-minute tour, offered weekdays, walks you through the state-of-the-art bottling plant and explains how wine is transferred from barrel to bottle.

Bocce Ball Courts

Adults and children alike can enjoy the four regulation bocce ball courts, set amid manicured lawns on the west side of the winery.

RUSTIC

Adorned with dark wooden floors and an Argentine grill, this restaurant *(below)* features mostly Italian dishes. More than 4,000 Italian olive oil tins line the walls. An outside terrace offers gorgeous views over the Alexander Valley.

The Art of Blending

Most wines produced today are done so blending a variety of wines from different barrels, grape varieties, vineyards, vintages, and/or plots. The goal is to combine the best qualities of each distinct wine, such as aroma, palette, or color. Blending requires experience and experimentation, plus the ability to anticipate how distinct flavors can be successfully integrated.

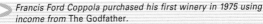
Francis Ford Coppola purchased his first winery in 1975 using income from The Godfather.

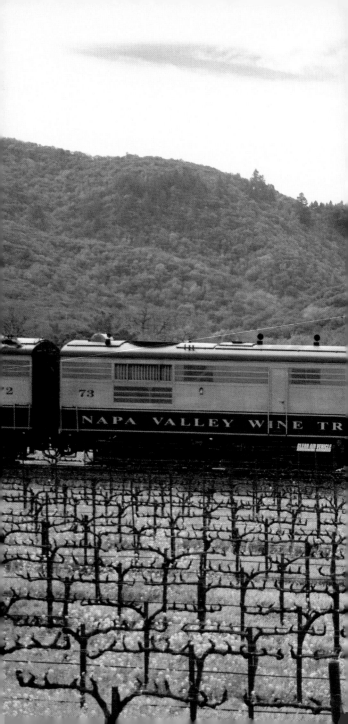

Left **Painting of wine-making equipment** Right **Pomo women gathering acorns**

🔟 Moments in History

First Inhabitants

The Wine Country region was originally populated by the Wappo and, further north, the Pomo. These sedentary hunter-gatherer cultures often went naked in summer and wore animal furs in winter. They were decimated by Mexican landlords, smallpox, and, later, by gold rush settlers.

Father Serra with Portola in San Diego

Missions Founded

The first Spanish mission in California was established in 1769 at San Diego, by explorer Gaspar de Portola and Father Junipero Serra. During the next 54 years, 20 other missions were founded to convert the local Indians to Christianity. They spanned 650 miles (1,040 km) along the El Camino Real from San Diego to modern-day Sonoma.

Bear Flag Revolt

On June 14, 1846, US settlers in Sonoma rebelled against Mexican rule. They raised a homemade flag with a white ground, emblazoned with a grizzly bear facing a red star. California was declared an independent republic. Nine days later, the U.S. Army occupied the region.

First Vines Planted

The first vines were planted in California in the late 18th century by Spanish missionaries. The cuttings were descended from black grapes brought to Mexico in 1520 by Hernán Cortés. The "Mission grape" was the dominant grape variety in California until the 20th century.

California's First Winery

In 1857, Hungarian immigrant Agoston Haraszthy (1812–69) established the Buena Vista Winery in Sonoma Valley after unsuccessfully experimenting with grape growing elsewhere in California. He published the *Report on Grapes and Wine of California* earning the nickname "Father of California Viticulture."

Railroad Built

Initiated in 1864, the Napa Valley Railroad was financed by magnate Samuel Brannan to bring passengers from a ferry landing at Soscol to his new spa resort at Calistoga, which it reached in 1868. Passenger service operated to Calistoga until 1928, after which the line was used solely for freight.

Phylloxera

The phylloxera epidemic that ravaged European vineyards in the 1850s originated in Californian vines that were shipped to England. Native North American species were partially resistant, but their grafting with European vines to produce the AxR1 rootstock led to their decimation by phylloxera in the 1980s.

Prohibition
On January 16, 1920, the 18th Amendment to the Constitution ushered in Prohibition, which banned the manufacture and sale of alcohol. Wineries survived by producing sacramental wines or table grapes. Only 140 wineries were in operation when Prohibition was repealed in 1933.

The Judgment of Paris
The world's view of California wines underwent a paradigm shift in 1976 when French judges at the blind Paris Wine Tasting event awarded top honors in both red and white categories to California wines pitted against the best of Bordeaux and Burgundy wines.

Napa Valley Wine Train Introduced
In 1987, a group of investors purchased the abandoned Southern Pacific rail line (originally built for the Napa Valley Railroad) and initiated the Napa Valley Wine Train on twice-daily dining tours between Napa and St. Helena. It has carried more than 2 million passengers since it began operation in 1989.

Pullman Rail car, Napa Valley Wine Train

Top 10 Famous People

1 Father Junipero Serra (1713–84)
A Franciscan friar, Serra founded the missions at San Diego and Carmel, where he is buried.

2 George Calvert Yount (1794–1865)
Yount was a trapper who settled in Napa Valley and planted the first vines.

3 Count Agoston Haraszthy (1812–69)
This Hungarian emigrant and writer founded the first commercial winery in California.

4 Robert Louis Stevenson (1850–94)
Famous Scottish novelist Stevenson wrote *The Silverado Squatters,* recalling his honeymoon at a mining camp on Mount St. Helena.

5 Josephine Tychson (1855–1939)
Born into an affluent family, she built the first female-owned winery in California.

6 Jack London (1876–1916)
The Jack London State Historic Park is named after this novelist and social activist *(see p78)*.

7 André Tchelistcheff (1901–94)
A Russian by birth, Tchelistcheff is called the "dean of American winemakers."

8 Robert Mondavi (1913–2008)
Pioneering wine-maker and wine industry ambassador, he helped put Napa on the map.

9 Mike Grgich (b. 1923)
His 1973 Chateau Montelena Chardonnay was named best white wine at the Judgment of Paris.

10 Francis Ford Coppola (b. 1939)
Hollywood producer Coppola owns his namesake family-friendly winery *(see pp30–31)*.

Left **Vineyards, Carneros region** Right **Wine samples, Stag's Leap Wine Cellars**

🔟 AVAs

Carneros

To the south of the Sonoma and Napa Valleys, the Carneros region of rolling meadows borders San Pablo Bay. Morning mists and cold winds make this one of the coolest appellations, perfect for Chardonnay and Pinot Noir, which make up the lion's share of varietals grown here. Grapes take longer to mature here, giving the wines greater subtlety and structure.

Rutherford

Spanning the width of Napa Valley, this AVA is the historical core of the valley and has some of the most fertile soils in the region, as well as many of the region's most celebrated wineries. It is given predominantly to growing Cabernet Sauvignon and produces muscular, well-balanced wines.

Oakville

Immediately south of Rutherford and likewise known for Cabernet Sauvignons, Oakville produces wines that are typically less robust and somewhat spicier than its neighbor. The slightly cooler climate also favors Chardonnay and Sauvignon Blanc. The AVA was put on the map in the 1960s by Robert Mondavi's famous vineyard.

Dry Creek Valley

Northwest of Healdsburg, this versatile AVA occupies a compact, narrow valley that produces varietals from Sauvignon Blanc to Semillon and Syrah, grown on small estates. Sangiovese is growing in popularity here as a preferred vine. Most of the wineries are strung along Dry Creek Road, making touring a breeze.

Wine estate, Dry Creek Valley

Stag's Leap District

This AVA, beneath the Vaca mountains on the east side of Napa Valley, leapt to fame when a Stag's Leap Cabernet Sauvignon won the Judgment of Paris *(see p13)*. The distinctive reddish soils produce velvety Cabernets whose elegance is often attributed to cool air that funnels in from San Pablo Bay.

Sonoma Valley

This AVA stretches north from San Pablo Bay to Santa Rosa. Many varietals grow well in the alluvial valley and volcanic mountainside soils of the narrow valley, which channels fog from the bay and gradually warms to the north.

Alexander Valley

Although one of the northernmost appellations in Sonoma County, this is also one of the hottest AVAs and combines rich alluvial soils with the ripening power of the sun to produce big, bold Zinfandels, Cabernet Sauvignons, and Merlots. Subtler wines are produced from grapes grown on the cooler hillsides.

Russian River Valley

The cool maritime air filtering up and over the valley dampens the grapes' sugar content and lends a subtlety and complexity to the wines produced here. Chardonnay and Pinot Noir dominate, and the region is acclaimed for producing some of the best Pinot Noirs in California. Zinfandels are also important.

Chardonnay grapes from Yountville

Yountville

The most southerly of Napa Valley red-wine AVAs and a patchwork combination of soils and climates, Yountville's cool climate and well-drained, loamy soils produce powerful Bordeaux-style reds. Several red and white varietals thrive here. Its famously high-tannin Cabernet Sauvignons age well.

Anderson Valley

This northern AVA extending up through Mendocino County along the Navarro River is influenced by a cool, foggy maritime climate, with wide diurnal temperature changes. Chardonnay, Riesling, and Gewürztraminers do well, and the region produces exceptional sparkling wines. Grapes are harvested later than in neighboring AVAs.

Left **An old grape press in Husch Winery, Mendocino** Right **Wine labels**

🔟 Stages in Wine Production

1 Pruning and Training
In January, vines are pruned to remove the previous year's growth and reduce the number of potential buds so as to produce more concentrated fruit. As buds sprout and flower, they are tied to training wires that guide the direction of growth.

2 Plowing and Planting
Plowing, which is done in March and April, helps aerate the soil and prepare it for planting of new vines from the nursery. Root vines are planted in early spring to absorb rainfall.

3 Summer Pruning
By July, fertilized flowers develop into berries, called the "fruit set." Producers of quality wines prune some of the immature grape bunches to reduce the vine's yield and concentrate its energy in the remaining grapes.

4 Harvesting
As grapes ripen, their sugar levels rise while acidity falls. The harvest, which usually begins in September or October, is timed for the moment when the two elements are in perfect balance. The ripe grape bunches are hand picked and placed, by tradition, in wicker baskets.

5 Crushing and Destemming
Grape bunches are fed into a machine that crushes the grapes between rollers. The grape juice is exposed to natural yeasts on the skins, although cultured yeast is often added to initiate fermentation. The juice drains through perforations that retain the stems, for easy removal.

6 Fermentation and Maceration
Yeast converts the grape's sugars into alcohol. The process produces heat, and temperatures in the fermentation tanks are carefully controlled for optimum results. Red wine fermentation takes up to one week; white wines take longer. Red wines gain their color from contact between grape juice and skins – known as maceration – during fermentation. White wines do not require skins, which are removed prior to fermentation.

Grape harvesting

Grape sugar gives wine its fruitiness and richness, while acidity gives it a liveliness on the palate.

Pressing
After the juice is transferred to a different container, the remaining solid mass of pulp and skin is pressed to produce a viscous "press wine," which may be added to the free-run juice during blending to increase color and tannin in red wines.

Wines maturing in oak barrels

Maturing
The juice is left to mature in air-tight, temperature-controlled stainless steel tanks. Oak barrels are preferred for quality wines, as the porous wood permits a gentle oxidation that helps soften tannins, increases the complexity of flavors, and can impart spicy or vanilla overtones to a wine.

Fining and Filtering
Suspended particles in wine barrels are removed by adding a binding agent, such as egg white, which attracts the sediments. The solid deposits fall to the bottom of the barrel and are filtered off, and the wine is transferred to a clean vessel to continue maturing.

Blending and Bottling
Wines from various casks or tanks will be blended to produce the desired wine. The process may also involve blending different types of grapes, and grapes grown on distinct vineyards. After additional filtering, the wine is bottled using systems that prevent contact with air.

Top 10 Wine Terms

Aroma
The smell of a wine, produced by its fruit and the type of grape.

Bouquet
A wine's scent resulting from the maturing process in the oak barrel and the aging process after bottling.

Estate Bottled
Wines made from grapes grown in the winery's own vineyards and in the same AVA as the winery.

Méthode Champenoise
The production of sparkling wine by adding yeast and sugar to bottled wine to induce secondary fermentation.

Oaky
A distinct and desirable taste or smell resulting from aging wines in oak barrels.

Tannin
A naturally occurring chemical in grape skins and wood barrels. It gives red wines structure.

Terroir
The combination of soil, slope, aspect, and climate of a specific region, resulting in a distinct flavor.

Varietal
A wine made from a particular type of grape and displaying the grape's distinct characteristics.

Vertical Tasting
Tasting a variety of wines from the same winery, starting from the youngest to the oldest.

Vintage
The year that grapes were harvested, as shown on the label of the bottle, which might not be available until several years later.

California Wine Country's Top 10

Discover more at www.dk.com

Left **Ferrari-Carano Vineyards** Center **Spring Mountain barrel room** Right **Castello di Amorosa**

🔟 Winery Tours

Robert Mondavi Winery

Founded in 1966 as Napa's first modern winery since Prohibition, this mission-style complex is regarded as a temple to viticulture, and draws huge crowds. It offers striking architecture, fine wines, and excellent winery tours *(see p71)*.

Spring Mountain Vineyard

This winery rises from the valley floor to almost the top of Spring Mountain. Famous as the set for the 1980s TV soap opera *Falcon Crest*, the winery's Germanic Victorian mansion is a highlight. The tour includes the vineyards, caves, and a horse-barn filled with wine-making artifacts. ◎ *2805 Spring Mountain Rd., St. Helena, 94574 • Map L3 • 707 967 4188 • Open 10am–4pm, by appointment • Adm • www.springmountainvineyard.com*

Sterling Vineyards

Inspired by Greek island architecture, this white hilltop winery stands atop a knoll and is

Aerial tram, Sterling Vineyards

reached by an aerial tram, which offers dramatic views. A tour of the winery follows elevated walkways lined with motion-sensitive informative screens *(see pp14–15)*.

Castello di Amorosa

A fantasy in stone, this winery is themed as a Tuscan castle. The state-of-the-art production facility, which makes award-winning wines, is tucked behind the castle. Visit mid-week, as hordes of weekend visitors flock to view the torture chamber and other recreations of medieval life *(see pp14–15)*.

Jarvis Winery

A small, intimate and little-known boutique winery, Jarvis has a natural spring waterfall in its vast underground cave – a terrific venue for an enlightening wine-tasting experience. The Vintage Tasting Tour with sit-down tasting is by appointment and includes six wines, including a Reserve label. Photography is discouraged in the caves. ◎ *2970 Monticello Rd., Napa, 94558 • Map M5 • 800 255 5280 • Adm • www.jarviswines.com*

Inglenook

This ostentatious ivy-clad winery is owned by Hollywood producer Francis Ford Coppola, whose

accomplishments are featured in museum displays that also trace the estate's history. Tastings are offered in a cavernous bar, and there is a free hour-long Legacy Tour. Formerly known as Rubicon Estates, the estate reverted to its original name in 2011 *(see p71)*.

Matanzas Creek Winery

Time a visit for May or June, when the barn-like winery's lavender fields – California's largest – are in full bloom. Matanzas Creek also has flower gardens and olive groves that are ideal for picnics. A store sells lavender items such as bath and spa products, and the airy winery interior is lined with art pieces *(see p82)*.

Ferrari-Carano Vineyards

Centered on a pink Italianate mansion, Ferrari-Carano has a huge vaulted cellar and two tasting rooms: a Mediterranean-style main room serving lesser priced wines, and the sumptuous Enoteca Lounge for reserve wines. Its expansive formal gardens, with arbors, sculptures, and fountains, are a riot of color in spring and summer *(see p89)*.

Schramsberg Vineyards

A visit to this winery, perched high on the wooded slopes of Diamond Mountain, would prove to be most rewarding *(see pp14–15)*. It specializes in sparkling wines. The compulsory tour, by appointment, includes its Victorian mansion, bottle-lined

Tasting room, Schramsberg Vineyards

caves, and a sit-down tasting. Robert Louis Stevenson recounts a visit in *The Silverado Squatters*.

Medlock Ames

Surrounded by rolling woodland, this young mountaintop winery set amid fragrant herb and vegetable gardens is reached by a long, winding dirt driveway. Built on several levels, with the natural slope, it produces gravity-fed wines without use of pumps. Pizzas are served alfresco from a wood-burning oven. A speakeasy bar inspired by the Gold Rush is an alternative to the stylish stone-and-steel tasting room. ◈ *3487 Alexander Valley Rd., Healdsburg, 95448 • Map H2 • 707 431 8845 • Open 10am–5pm • Adm • www.medlockames.com*

Left **Tasting room, Beaulieu vineyards** Right **Frog's Leap winery**

TOP 10 Grape Varieties

Chardonnay
Considered the king of white wine grapes, this variety accounts for about a quarter of all wine made in California. Different wine-making practices can produce chardonnays that vary in style, although many California Chardonnays are sweet and buttery due to excessive oaking.

Sauvignon Blanc
Originating in France, this important white wine grape is known for producing crisp, aromatic wines, often with aromas of herbs or even grass. Warmer climates produce a more robust wine with flavors that hint of tropical fruits. In California, it is typically blended with Semillon.

Cabernet Sauvignon
The most important red wine varietal in California, Cabernet Sauvignon grapes produce full-bodied wines in hot climates, but also deliver lighter wines in mountain zones. Blackberry and blackcurrant are telltale aromas.

Petite Sirah

Zinfandel
This variety produces bunches with individual grapes that vary in size and ripeness. Overripe grapes with high sugar alcohol levels produce tannic wines, while cooler terroirs produce subtle Zinfandels with berry and cherry flavors, often used for pink rosés.

Petite Sirah
A long-lived and sturdy red wine varietal whose small berries and high skin-to-juice ratio are known for producing wines with intense fruit and pepper flavors, Petite Sirah is normally blended with Zinfandels to tone down the latter's "jammy" qualities.

Syrah
This red wine varietal produces deep maroon wines displaying flavors of black pepper and chocolate. Cooler areas of California produce wines typical of France's Rhône region. Hotter climates produce full-bodied wines often referred to as Shiraz.

Riesling
Of German origin, the Riesling grape grows well in cooler

Clusters of Cabernet Sauvignon grapes

Several hundred grape varieties exist, many of them hybrids.

climates such as the Anderson Valley of Mendocino. Lightness combined with fruity flavours, complex aromas, and high acidity are key to this varietal's popularity. The grape also produces delicious dessert wines.

Pinot Noir
A varietal that grows well in cooler parts of the Wine Country, Pinot Noir's complex flavor communicates the unique terroir qualities better than any other grape. Many of California's best champagnes use this grape.

Pinot Noir vines

Merlot
A red-wine grape second only to Cabernet Sauvignon in acreage planted in California, Merlot produces a medium-bodied wine. Skilled wine-makers can craft it into highly structured wines. Merlot grapes are often blended with Cabernet Sauvignon for a well-balanced color and bouquet.

Sangiovese
An Italian varietal, Sangiovese was introduced to California by 19th-century immigrants but has become popular only in recent years. It produces slightly spicy young wines with hints of strawberry. Older wines aged in barrels can have a pronounced oaky quality.

Top 10 Vintages

1 Shafer Hillside Select
A Cabernet Sauvignon from the Stag's Leap AVA, it is aged for four years before release.

2 B.R. Cohn "Silver Label" Cabernet Sauvignon
A complex blend of grapes from various B.R. Cohn vineyards, it has hints of black cherry and vanilla.

3 Ferrari-Carano Mountain Grown Sangiovese
A limited production, full and fruity wine from the Alexander Valley.

4 Seghesio Zinfandel
Blended from Alexander and Dry Creek Valley grapes, this oak-aged wine is supple and spicy.

5 Grgich Hills Chardonnay
An acidic and well-balanced Chardonnay with aromas of honey and baked pear.

6 Kistler Vineyards Chardonnay
This wine's richness and texture combine to produce a lingering bouquet of apricot, honeysuckle, and exotic spices.

7 Williams Selyen Pinot Noir
This perfectly balanced wine has a nose of cherry and raspberries.

8 Robert Mondavi Cabernet Sauvignon Reserve
This classic wine has aromas of cedarwood and crème de cassis.

9 Rosenblum Cellars Vintner's Cuvée Zinfandel
A spicy, inexpensive wine with a bouquet of cedar and plum, and a blackberry palate.

10 Stag's Leap Cabernet
This distinctive Cabernet has a superb balance of aroma, tannin, and flavor.

Particular winery vintages can vary significantly from the same wine from another year.

Left **Pacific Coast Air Museum** Right **Napa Valley Museum**

🔟 Museums and Galleries

1 Charles M. Schulz Museum

Tucked away in a residential district of northwest Santa Rosa, this spacious and modern museum delights visitors with its exhibits of the artist's life and his most famous creations, Charlie Brown and Snoopy the dog (see p24).

Snoopy, Charles M. Schulz Museum

2 Sharpsteen Museum

Initiated by former Hollywood producer Ben Sharpsteen, this quaint and quirky museum focuses on northern California history since its settlement by the Wappo people. Exhibits include a restored stagecoach, a 3D diorama of early Calistoga, and a cottage that was originally part of Calistoga's Hot Springs Resort. ◈ 1311 Washington St., Calistoga, 94515 • Map K2 • 707 942 5911 • Open 11am–4pm • Adm • www.sharpsteen-museum.org

3 Sonoma County Museum

Housed in the former Federal-style main post office, which was relocated here in 1979, this museum regales the history of Sonoma County with rotating displays. It also has a permanent collection by world-famous artist duo Christo and Jean-Claude (see p24).

4 Clos Pegase Winery

Post-Modernist architect Michael Graves designed this eye-catching, avant-garde winery as a "temple to wine and art." Contemporary sculptures by world-renowned artists such as Henry Moore, Richard Serra, and Sir Anthony Caro dot the grounds, while the winery's massive underground cave hosts European statuary dating back to the 17th century (see pp14–15).

Diorama of early Calistoga, Sharpsteen Museum

Robert Louis Stevenson Silverado Museum
Novelist Robert Louis Stevenson is honored at this museum, which displays original manuscripts and personal artifacts. The manuscripts include *The Silverado Squatters*, chronicling the author's travels in Napa Valley in 1880. ◎ *1490 Library Ln., St. Helena, 94574 • Map L3 • 707 963 3757 • Open noon–4pm Tue–Sat • www.silveradomuseum.org*

Robert Louis Stevenson Museum

Di Rosa Preserve
More than 2,000 works of contemporary art are displayed throughout this 217-acre (89-ha) wine estate. The whimsical artistic wonderland includes a car that hangs from a tree, and a colorful cow seemingly walking atop a large lake. ◎ *5200 Sonoma Hwy., Napa, 94559 • Map L5 • 707 226 5991 • Open 10am–6pm Wed–Sun (Nov–Mar: to 4pm); tour required • Adm (suggested donation) • www.dirosaart.org*

The Hess Collection
Considered one of the world's finest private art collections, the Hess Collection displays work by such internationally prominent names as Andy Goldsworthy, and Frank Stella *(see pp8–11)*.

Pacific Coast Air Museum
Founded in 1989, this museum *(see p80)* displays more than 30 historic U.S. military aircraft. Prize exhibits include a Vietnam-era Huey helicopter, an F-4 Phantom, a Hawker Harrier Jump Jet, and an F-15 Eagle. It hosts aviation-themed exhibits, and organizes the Wings Over Wine Country Air Show in August.

Napa Valley Museum
The exhibits here range from the valley's geological origins and American Indian life to the modern wine industry. There's also an interactive exhibit on the science of wine-making. ◎ *55 Presidents Circle, Yountville, 94599 • Map L4 • 707 944 0500 • Open 10am–4pm Tue–Sun • Adm • www. napavalleymuseum.org*

Healdsburg Museum
This museum profiles northern Sonoma County's American Indian roots and Victorian heyday. The neoclassical building is surrounded by Victorian homes. ◎ *221 Matheson St., Healdsburg, 95448 • Map H2 • 707 431 3325 • Open 11am–4pm Wed–Sun • www.healdsburgmuseum.org*

Left **Tables set for lunch, Napa Valley Wine Auction** Right **Music in the Vineyards**

🔟 Festivals and Holidays

Mustard, Mud, and Music Festival

Local jazz combos perform live at venues throughout Calistoga during this weekend event. It has traditionally been an integral part of the erstwhile Napa Valley International Mustard Festival.
◈ *Early Mar • www.mustardfestival.com/mustard-music-mud.html*

Barrel-Tasting Weekend

Heralding the arrival of wine season, wineries and wine-tasting rooms throughout the Russian River and Alexander Valley regions offer a sneak taste of barrel wine that has yet to be bottled. ◈ *Mar • www.wineroad.com/annualevents*

Barrel-Tasting Weekend

Napa Valley Wine Festival

In Yountville during May, wineries and restaurants from throughout the region adopt individual schools and combine their talents and products to raise funds. ◈ *May • http://nvef.org*

Napa Valley Wine Auction

Held at the Meadowood Resort *(see p63)*, this event draws the A-list of Wine Country figures. The auction raises millions of dollars for charity. The few general public tickets sell out early. ◈ *Jun • www.napavintners.com/anv*

Napa County Fair and Fireworks

The Calistoga Fairgrounds hosts this four-day event, held the week of July 4. Although its main focus is ostensibly wine, the fair also has animal husbandry exhibits, live music, strolling entertainers, and a July 4 Parade plus fireworks. ◈ *Week of 4 Jul • www.napacountyfair.org*

Music in the Vineyards

This three-week-long celebration of chamber music hosts twilight concerts at some of the finest venues throughout Napa Valley. Acclaimed musicians from North America and Europe interlace their virtuoso performances with witty repartee. ◈ *Aug • www.musicinthevineyards.org*

Gravenstein Apple Fair

The town of Sebastopol hosts this fair. Gravenstein apples and apple products, plus arts and crafts, are sold, and children can enjoy hayrides and storytelling. Live entertainment, cooking demonstrations, and a petting zoo are other attractions. ⌖ *Mid–Aug • http://gravensteinapplefair.com*

Gravenstein Apple Fair

Sonoma Wine Country Weekend

This epicurean Labor Day Weekend event entails wine-maker lunches, dinner parties, wine–food pairings, and cooking demonstrations. More than 170 wineries present their latest and Reserve wines. The event culminates the Sonoma Valley Harvest Wine Auction. ⌖ *Sep • www.sonomawinecountryweekend.com*

Russian River Jazz and Blues Festival

A fun-filled event during the weekend after Labor Day, this festival *(see pp26–7)* celebrates summer with live jazz concerts on the banks of the Russian River. Rent a deck chair or inner tube and laze in the sun while some of the world's best jazz performers entertain.

Sonoma County Harvest Fair

Celebrating the wine harvest in the Sonoma County Fairgrounds, this festival draws thousands of visitors for farm animal competitions, rodeo, rides, live music, and more. More than 150 local wineries display their wines. The World Championship Grape Stomp is a highlight. ⌖ *Three days Sep–Oct • www.harvestfair.org*

Top 10 Cultural Experiences

1 St. Helena Public Library
Its Napa Wine Library details wine-making in the valley. ⌖ *1492 Library Ln., St. Helena, 94574 • Map L3*

2 Tuesdays in the Plaza
Free summer concerts are hosted on Tuesday evenings. ⌖ *Healdsburg Av. & Plaza St., Healdsburg, 95448 • Map H2*

3 Sonoma County Wine Library
This is a great place to learn about the county's wine history. ⌖ *139 Piper St., Healdsburg, 95448 • Map L5*

4 Bacchus Glass Studio
Watch master glass blower Frank Cavaz craft unique works of art. ⌖ *21707 8th St. E., Sonoma, 95476 • Map L5*

5 Falcon Crest
Relive the 1980s television soap opera at Spring Mountain Vineyard *(see p40)*, the setting for *Falcon Crest.*

6 Movie Gallery
The Francis Ford Coppola Winery displays the director's Oscars *(see pp30–31).*

7 Infineon Raceway
Motorsports fans are treated to track testing and races daily. ⌖ *29355 Arnold Dr., Sonoma, 95476 • Map L5*

8 Napa Valley Opera House
An 1880 Italianate building hosting music performances, as well as theater *(see p53).*

9 Wells Fargo Center for the Arts
Performances here span the spectrum from ballet to rock. ⌖ *50 Mark West Springs Rd., Santa Rosa, 95403 • Map J3*

10 Chamber Music in Napa Valley
Hosted at wineries and other venues, this winter series features top chamber ensembles. ⌖ *625 Randolph St., Napa, 94559 • Map M5*

California Wine Country's Top 10

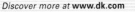

Left **Canoeing on the Russian River** Right **Bicycling, Silverado Trail**

Outdoor Activities

Bicycling
Wine Country's back roads have routes to satisfy both leisurely sightseers and hard-core cyclists. The many backcountry parks also offer terrain perfect for mountain biking. ❧ *Getaway Adventures: 2228 Northpoint Pkwy. Santa Rosa, 95407* • www.getawayadventures.com

Glider Rides
Soaring in a glider provides the ultimate view and is one of the most exhilarating ways to experience Wine Country. Several companies offer rides, including introductory lessons. ❧ *Crazy Creek Adventures* • www.crazycreekairadventures.com

Ballooning
Hot-air balloons offer spectacular views over the valley. Rides begin around sunrise, and end with a traditional champagne toast *(see p70)*.

River Cruise
To get another perspective on Wine Country, take the Dolphin Charters' *Delphinus*. It journeys from Vallejo, on San Pablo Bay, and up the Napa River, passing the Carneros AVA vineyards. ❧ *Dolphin Charters: 1007 Leneve Place El Cerrito, 94530* • www.dolphincharters.com

Hiking
More than a dozen state parks in California tempt hikers and offer possibilities, from easy walks to challenging multi-day backpack hikes. The Napa Sierra Club welcomes non-members to join its guided hikes. ❧ *www.redwood.sierraclub.org/napa*

Canoeing
Paddling the Russian River is a popular activity on warm summer days. Canoes and kayaks can be rented around Healdsburg and Guerneville.

Hot-air ballooning

Burke's Canoe Trips *(see pp26–7)* offers self-guided 10-mile (16-km) trips from May to mid-October.

7 Camping

Pack a tent or rent a recreational vehicle (RV) for overnight stays beneath the redwoods. Reservations are required at California state parks ($17–32), and are advisable for private campgrounds.

Campground at Hendy Woods State Park

8 Horseback Riding

Explore the Wine Country on horseback on bridal paths that lace many state parks, granting access to the forests and mountains. The Triple Creek Horse Outfit offers guided tours on the Kunde Family Estate Winery. Ⓢ *Triple Creek Horse Outfit: 11011 Sonoma Hwy., Kenwood, 95452 • www.triplecreekhorseoutfit.com*

9 Kayaking

The Napa River, which wends a 50-mile (80-km) journey from Mount St. Helena to the San Pablo Bay, is tailored for kayaking. Kayak Napa Valley offers guided trips in season. Ⓢ *www.kayaknv.com*

10 Skydiving in Cloverdale

For the ultimate thrill, don a jumpsuit and harness, and charge toward the Russian River at 120 mph (193 kmph). NorCal Skydiving offers tandem skydiving packages. Ⓢ *NorCal Skydiving: Chrome Iron Rd,, Cloverdale, 95425 • www.norcalskydiving.com*

Top 10 Nature Trails

1 Bald Mountain Vista Loop
A climbing trail that loops around Sugarloaf Ridge State Park. Ⓢ *2605 Adobe Canyon Rd., Kenwood, 95452 • Map L4*

2 Bothe-Napa Valley State Park Trail
A 4.5-mile (7-km) loop through redwood forests with a few steep sections. Ⓢ *3801 Hwy. 29, Calistoga, 94515 • Map K3*

3 Napa River Ecological Reserve
The single trail here extends along the forested riverbank. Ⓢ *Yountville Crossroad, Yountville, 94558 • Map L4*

4 Mount St. Helena
This summit trail begins in Robert Louis Stevenson State Park. Ⓢ *3801 St. Helena Hwy., Calistoga, 94515 • Map K2*

5 Hood Mountain Trail
This fire road in the Mayacamas Mountains climbs to the summit of Mt. Hood. Ⓢ *3000 Los Alamos Rd., Santa Rosa, 95409 • Map K3*

6 Cloverdale River Park
A stretch of the Russian River reached from Cloverdale. Ⓢ *31820 McCray Rd., Rohnert Park, 94925 • Map G1*

7 Sonoma Overlook Trail
This gentle loop offers sensational views. Ⓢ *First St. W. and Mountain Overlook Trail, Sonoma, 95476 • Map K3*

8 Bay Area Ridge Trail
Within Jack London State Historic Park, this hike gains 1,500 ft (457 m) elevation. Ⓢ *2400 London Ranch Rd., Glen Ellen, 95442 • Map K4*

9 Colonel Armstrong Loop
This trail takes in the best of Armstrong Redwoods. Ⓢ *17000 Armstrong Woods Rd., Guerneville, 95446 • Map G3*

10 Hermit Huts and Little Hendy
Within Hendy Woods Park, this trail runs through a stand of redwoods. Ⓢ *Greenwood Rd., Philo, 95466 • Map A2*

Left **Mount St. Helena** Center **Armstrong Redwoods State Reserve** Right **Petrified Forest**

Natural Sights

1 Napa River

With its headwaters on Mount St. Helena, this river runs south through the Napa Valley and empties into San Pablo Bay. The estuarine lower section from the town of Napa southward can be explored by canoe and on boat trips. Wading birds pick among the marshes and sloughs. ✪ *Map M5*

2 Lake Sonoma

This lake lies at the heart of a 17,615-acre (7,129-ha) park that serves hikers, horseback riders, and mountain bikers with more than 40 miles (64 km) of trails. ✪ *Map G1 • Milt Brandt Visitor Center: 707 433 9483*

Lake Sonoma

3 Bothe-Napa Valley State Park

Located to the north of St. Helena, this natural forest reserve is one of the most easily accessed parks in Wine Country, and is popular for picnics and camping. Its mostly level hiking trails weave through fern glens and stands of Douglas fir and coastal redwoods. A swimming pool is open on weekdays. ✪ *3801 Hwy. 29, Calistoga, 94515 • Map K3 • 707 942 4575 • Open 8am–sunset • Adm • www.parks.ca.gov*

4 Harbin Hot Springs

A Mecca for holistic treatments, this new age retreat is centered on natural hot springs in a peaceful mountain setting. Massages and other treatments are offered, as is yoga, and the clothing-optional thermal pools are a perfect treat after vigorous hikes along trails that lead into the surrounding hills. Guests below 18 years of age must be accompanied by an adult. ✪ *18424 Harbin Springs Rd., Middletown, 95461 • Map K1 • 707 987 2477 • Open 24 hrs • Adm • www.harbin.org*

5 Napa River Ecological Reserve

Some 150 species of native birds and animals find shelter in the meadows and in the shade of willows, oaks, and other habitats that line the watercourse in the Napa River Ecological Reserve. A mile-long trail offers easy access *(see pp18–19)*.

Kayaking at Lake Berryessa

Old Faithful Geyser of California

Erupting like clockwork about every 30 minutes, this hot-spring geyser spouts boiling water up to 100 ft (30 m) in the air. The scalding pool is surrounded by marsh grasses and stands of California palms. The geyser often "predicts" impending earthquakes by changing its rhythm and strength *(see p14)*.

Petrified Forest

One of the finest examples of a Pliocene fossil forest in the world, this park preserves fallen redwood trees dating back 3 million years, when a volcanic eruption felled the trees and buried them with ash. Now turned to stone, many are as long as 65 ft (20 m). ꙮ *4100 Petrified Forest Rd., Calistoga, 94515 • Map K3 • 707 942 6667 • Open 9am–5pm • Adm • www.petrifiedforest.org*

Mount St. Helena

Rising above surrounding peaks in the Mayacamas Mountains, this volcanic peak (4,304 ft/1,312 m) was formed about 2.4 million years ago. Beginning in Robert Louis Stevenson State Park *(see p49)*, a steep trail to the summit offers a hike rewarded by fabulous views over Napa Valley and as far as the Pacific Ocean. ꙮ *Hwy. 29 • Map K2 • 707 942 4575 • Open 10am–5:30pm • www.parks.ca.gov*

Lake Berryessa

The largest lake in Napa County, this reservoir provides much of the water that irrigates Napa Valley. Some 15 miles (25 km) long by 3 miles (5 km) wide, it is popular for water-skiing, kayaking, and other recreation. Ducks, geese, and other waterfowl can be viewed from wildlife observation points. ꙮ *5520 Knoxville Rd., Napa, 94558 • Map M2 • 707 966 2111 • Open during summer • www.usbr.gov/mp/ccao/berryessa*

Armstrong Redwoods State Natural Reserve

One of the most majestic groves of coast redwoods in northern California, this peaceful reserve is laced by self-guided nature trails that wind beneath giant trees up to 310 ft (94.5 m) tall. The reserve has a visitor center, campsites, and picnic facilities *(see p27)*.

Left **Mission San Francisco Solano** Center **Bale Grist Mill** Right **Napa Valley Opera House**

TOP 10 Historic Sites

The Rhine House

The Rhine House
A Napa Valley icon, this extravagant building *(see p68)* on the Beringer Winery estate was built in 1884 as the home of German immigrant Frederick Beringer, who, with his brother Jacob, founded Beringer Vineyards in 1876. The 17-room Victorian mansion, reminiscent of the family's old German Rhineland home, features gables, turrets, stained-glass windows, and ornaments.

Bale Grist Mill
Named for its original owner, Dr Turner Bale, this water-powered grist mill was built in 1846 so that Napa Valley settlers could grind wheat into flour. The mill and its 36-ft (11-m) waterwheel remained in use

until the early 1900s. ✎ *3369 St. Helena Hwy., St. Helena, 94574 • Map K3 • 707 942 4575 • www.parks.ca.gov*

Luther Burbank Home & Gardens
The historic Burbank home, where horticulturalist Luther Burbank (1849–1926) lived and conducted his world-famous genetic experiments, is today a museum maintained by the city of Santa Rosa. It includes Burbank's modified Greek Revival house; a carriage house with exhibits relating to his life and work; and his greenhouse stocked with tools *(see p78)*.

Mission San Francisco Solano
Founded in 1823 and completed in 1832 as the last and most northerly of California's 21 missions, San Francisco Solano was secularized in 1834, fell into ruins, and was virtually destroyed in the 1906 earthquake. Restored in 1913, it is a part of Sonoma State Historic Park *(see pp20–21)*.

Jack London State Historic Park
Named for the writer and adventurer Jack London (1876–1916), this park is centered on the home that he built here in 1905 on what was then his Beauty Ranch. Trails lead through woodland to a cottage, lake, bathhouse, and the remains of "Wolf House," destroyed by fire in 1913 *(see p78)*.

Lachryma Montis

General Mariano Vallejo's former estate *(see pp22–3)*, half-a-mile (0.8 km) northwest of Sonoma Plaza, is a key site within Sonoma State Historic Park. The park's visitor center occupies the former warehouse. It stands

Lachryma Montis

beside Vallejo's two-story, wood-frame home which is furnished with his original possessions. ◎ Map L5

Greystone Cellars

This stately and iconic three-story stone edifice rising over Hwy 29 north of St. Helena was initiated in 1889 as the largest winery in California. The castle-like building was constructed with iron reinforcing rods to withstand earthquakes. Today, it serves as the Culinary Institute of America *(see p16)*.

Napa Valley Opera House

Locals take pride in their Italianate opera house, which opened in 1880 to a performance of Gilbert and Sullivan's *H.M.S. Pinafore*. It was restored in the 1990s and reopened in 2003 as a centerpiece of Napa's revitalization. It hosts live performances, from chorale to children's theater. ◎ 1030 Main St., Napa, 94559 • Map P5 • 707 226 7372 • www.nvoh.org

Napa Mill

The historic riverfront Napa Mill, in the city of Napa, originally served as a wharfside warehouse. Today the restored red-brick structure, which is listed on the National Register of Historical Places, hosts fine-dining restaurants, retail shops, a spa, and hotel. Outdoor concerts and events are held at the Riverbend Performance Plaza *(see p70)*.

Sebastiani Theatre

Rising over the east side of Sonoma Plaza, this Art Deco masterpiece helps preserve the plaza's historical charm. It was built as a movie house in 1933 by August Sebastiani, son of Samuele Sebastiani, who founded Sebastiani Vineyards in 1904. It still functions as a cinema and live entertainment venue *(see p80)*.

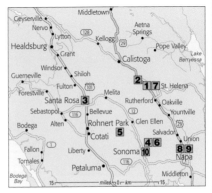

Left **Cannon on display at Fort Ross** Right **Mendocino as seen from the bay**

🔟 Wine Country Excursions

Clear Lake
At the heart of Clear Lake State Park, this freshwater lake is California's largest. The shores are a nesting site for waterfowl and the visitor center has exhibits on the ancient lifestyle of the Pomo American Indians *(see p99)*.

Suisun Bay
Surrounded by the largest marsh in California – Peytonia Slough – this tidal estuary has nature trails good for birding. Sunset Bay Kayaks has kayak trips through the slough. A "mothball" fleet of retired U.S. Navy vessels, including the USS Iowa, is anchored in the bay.
⬥ www.sunsetbaykayaks.com

Napa Valley Wine Train
One of Napa Valley's premier draws, this train combines a tour between downtown Napa and St. Helena with an excellent dining and wine-tasting experience *(see pp12–13)*.

Vallejo
The highlights of Vallejo include its 1869 Starr Mansion, the Mare Island Historic Park, plus dozens of National Historic Landmark buildings. The Vallejo Naval and Historical Museum recalls the city's 150-year-old association with the U.S. Navy.
⬥ Map M6 • Mare Island Historic Park, Railroad Av. & 8th St., Mare Island • 707 557 1538 • Open 10am–2pm Mon–Fri, 1st & 3rd Sat & Sun of month 10am–4pm

Mendocino
The quintessential California coast town of the 1850s, with clapboard-style Victorian houses, Mendocino enjoys a spectacular cliff-top setting. The visitor center and museum are in the historic Ford House. ⬥ Ford House, 735 Main St., Mendocino, 95460 • 707 937 5397 • Open 11am–4pm • www.mendocino.com

Point Reyes National Seashore
This national park protects a section of coast that is geologically separated from the continental U.S. by the San Andreas Fault. Attractions include sweeping beaches, rocky headlands, marshy estuaries teeming with wildlife, a Tule elk reserve, and a historic lighthouse. ⬥ 1 Bear Valley Rd. • Map H6 • www.nps.gov/pore/index.htm

Napa Valley Wine Train

Completed in 1870, the Point Reyes Lighthouse stands at what is regarded to be the windiest, foggiest place on the U.S. west coast.

7 Skunk Train

This heritage railroad offers a tour through the coast mountain redwoods between Fort Bragg and Willits. Initially a logging railroad, the 40-mile (64-km) track crosses 30 bridges and trestles and passes through two mountain tunnels. 🖰 www.skunktrain.com

Bodega Bay

8 Bodega Bay

Famous as the setting for Alfred Hitchcock's 1963 movie, *The Birds*, this fishing village has a birds-themed visitor center. The peninsula that shelters the bay is an ideal point for whale watching December through April. Sonoma Coast State Beach extends north for 8 miles (13 km). 🖰 *Map G5*
• www.bodegabay.com

9 Jenner

This small coastal village occupies a Pacific Ocean bluff at the mouth of the Russian River. Seals often haul out on the beach at Goat Rock State Park. Riptides here mean swimming is ill-advised. 🖰 *Map G3*

10 Fort Ross

Founded in 1812, Fort Ross was the southernmost Russian settlement in North America. It functioned as an agricultural supply base for Russia's Alaskan settlements. The wooden fort and stockade have been restored, and visitors can tour a replica chapel, barracks, and other buildings. 🖰 www.parks.ca.gov

Top 10 Beaches

1 Salmon Beach
This beach is popular for picnics and surfing. 🖰 *Bodega Bay • Map G4*

2 Stinson Beach
A 3-mile (5-km) long beach, good for fishing, surfing, and watching seals. 🖰 www.parksconservancy.org/visit/park-sites/stinson-beach.html

3 Goat Rock Beach
Seals often bask in the sun on this gray-sand beach at the mouth of the Russian River. 🖰 *Sonoma Coast State Park, Jenner • Map G3*

4 Shell Beach
Beneath rugged headlands, this beach has a dramatic setting. 🖰 *Sonoma Coast State Park, Jenner • Map G3*

5 Pebble Beach
Having shallow waters, this small public beach is popular for Abalone (sea snail) diving. 🖰 *Sea Ranch, 10 miles (16 km) north of Fort Ross*

6 Johnson's Beach
On the Russian River, this beach can get crowded with picnickers on summer weekends. 🖰 *Map G3*

7 Salt Point State Beach
This beach has rugged cliffs and coves, with pygmy forest growing atop headlands. 🖰 *Jenner • Map G3*

8 The Great Beach
Arcing for 11 miles (17 km), this sweep of wind-swept sand is pounded by dangerous surf. 🖰 *Point Reyes National Seashore • Map H6*

9 Drakes Beach, Point Reyes
Backed by sandstone cliffs, Drakes Beach has a café and visitor center. 🖰 *Point Reyes National Seashore • Map H6*

10 Van Damme State Beach
Inland of this beach, a boardwalk nature trail leads through pygmy forest atop the headland. 🖰 *3 miles (5 km) south of Mendocino*

Left **Angèle restaurant** Right **Mustards Grill**

🔟 Places to Eat

1 Market

Stone walls and a polished dark-wood bar that came from the Palace Hotel in San Francisco set a sophisticated tone at this moderately priced pub-restaurant in the heart of St. Helena. Chef-owner Eduardo Martínez conjures up delicious comfort food from market-fresh products. ⓢ *1347 Main St., St. Helena, 94574 • Map L3 • 707 963 3799 • Open 11:30am–9pm Mon–Thu, 11:30am–10pm Fri & Sat, 10am–9pm Sun • $$$$*

2 Zin Restaurant & Wine Bar

Zin is a favorite for casual fine dining, thanks to its eclectic seasonal menu of American classic dishes focusing on local fresh ingredients, many

Interior, **Zin Restaurant & Wine Bar**

pulled straight from the restaurant's own garden. Hearty Zin wines accompany meatloaf, grilled lamb chops, and heaps of garlic mashed potatoes, enjoyed in minimalist surrounds *(see p95).*

3 Angèle

In the historic 1890 ship's chandlery on the Napa riverfront, Angèle's bar-brick walls and timber beamed roof evoke the traditional ambience of a French country brasserie. Opt for the main dining room, bar, or riverside terrace to enjoy French bistro fare such as pâtés and bœuf bourguignon, plus seasonal salads *(see p75).*

4 LaSalette

Michelin inspectors have said this restaurant offers the "best hidden culinary value" in the Bay Area. New Portuguese cuisine combines southern European flavors, exotic spices, seafood, and fresh California produce *(see p85).*

5 Mustards Grill

A stone's throw north of Yountville, Mustards Grill has been a Napa Valley institution for three decades. Billing itself as an upscale truckstop diner, it serves sophisticated globe-spanning dishes including classic American fare and such specialtes as seared ahi tuna, and BBQ baby-back ribs *(see p75).*

Preceding pages **Mustard blooms in a vineyard, Healdsburg**

6 The French Laundry

Housed in a 19th-century former saloon, this French-California restaurant is considered one of the top restaurants in the country thanks to

The French Laundry

owner-chef Thomas Keller's creative genius and sublime execution. Diners get a choice of two nine-course tasting menus costing $270 per person; sittings can last for 4 hours *(see p75)*.

7 ZuZu

Small and cozy, this tapas restaurant in Napa's revitalized downtown district has an atmospheric feel, enhanced by the décor: exposed red-brick walls, aged wood beams, faded colonial floor tiles, and a weathered Mexican tin ceiling. Its menu features Mediterranean and Californian tapas made using organic and sustainable produce, seafood and meats *(see p75)*.

8 Redd

Acclaimed executive chef and owner of Redd, Richard Reddington serves an updated wine country cuisine with influences from Asia, Europe, and Mexico in a relaxed yet elegant environment. *A la carte* and tasting menus for lunch and dinner show off his signature blend of rich tastes that pairs well with wine from the deep cellar *(see p95)*.

9 Petite Syrah

This elegant "industrial"-style restaurant in the charming historic Railroad Square district has gained national stature for its soul-satisfying comfort food that celebrates the best of Sonoma County. The monthly menu might include Sonoma County foie gras with caramelized rhubarb, or grilled T-bone steak with fried crayfish and truffled baked potato *(see p85)*.

10 Applewood Inn

Tucked upstairs at the secluded Applewood Inn, this cozy and romantic Michelin starred restaurant recalls a French farmhouse, where diners look down on to a courtyard. The cuisine weds French influences with California ingredients, such as halibut with braised artichoke and wild mushroom ragout. Applewood also hosts special event dinners. ✆ *13555 California 116, Guerneville, 95446* • *Map G3* • *707 869 9093* • *Open 5:30–9:30pm Wed–Sun* • *$$$*

Left **St. Helena Olive Oil Company** Center **Picnic at V. Sattui Winery** Right **Wine and cheese**

🔟 Culinary Highlights

1 Sonoma Certified Farmers' Market
Held year-round, this market hosts dozens of local farmers, growers, and merchants selling fruit, vegetables, artisan breads, cheeses, and more. ◎ *Depot Park, 1st St. W., Sonoma, 95476 • Map L5 • 707 538 7023 • Open 9am–12:30pm Fri*

2 Picnic at V. Sattui Winery
Picnicking is the *raison d'être* at this small, family-owned, Tuscan-style winery on Hwy 29. The broad lawns have picnic tables and benches, and the deli is unsurpassed for its wide range of epicurean delights *(see p73)*.

3 Oxbow Public Market
This airy, state-of-the-art facility in downtown Napa hosts dozens of food outlets, including a butcher shop, fishmongers, fresh produce sellers, plus cafés and restaurants. There's live music on Friday nights, plus butchery and cooking classes *(see p70)*.

Oxbow Public Market, Napa town

4 Culinary Institute of America
The world's premier culinary college has two restaurants where visitors can sample food prepared by students. The Wine Spectator Restaurant offers a range of culinary experiences, while the Williams Center for Flavor Discovery acts as a café-restaurant *(see pp16–17)*.

5 Cooking Class at Ramekins
Ramekins is a B&B inn better known for its culinary school, where guest celebrity chefs offer cooking classes. Longer, intensive "Culinary Camps" demonstrate advanced techniques, while renowned sommeliers and wine-makers teach about wine-tasting and food pairing. ◎ *450 W Spain St., Sonoma, 95476 • Map L5 • 707 933 0450*

6 Family Table at Seghesio Family Vineyard
This tasting (held Friday to Sunday only) begins with a tour of the winery, followed by wine and food pairings in which five appetizer-size recipes are matched to limited release wines. ◎ *700 Grove St., Healdsburg, 95448 • Map H2 • 707 433 3579 • www.seghesio.com*

7 Wine and Cheese Pairing
Wine and cheese bring out the best in each

The Philo Apple farm grows about 60 varieties of apples (See p101).

other, hence they're tasted together. Creamy cheeses are best paired with acidic wines, whereas harder cheeses fare best with more tannic and hearty red wines. Blue and salty cheeses taste well with sweet wines.

Wine and cheese pairing

Tasting Olive Oils
The production of olive oil has exploded in Wine Country in recent years. Gourmet extra virgin olive oils offer a wide range of flavors. To learn the art of appreciation, visit the St. Helena Olive Oil Company *(see p70)*.

Vella Cheese Company
Founded in 1931 and housed in a sturdy stonewalled structure built in 1904, this company makes artisanal hand-cut cheese, from various award-winning Jacks and Cheddars to Swiss and Italian-style cheese. The store sells packaged cheese and gift boxes. ✪ *315 2nd St. E., Sonoma, 95476 • Map L5 • www.vellacheese.com*

Flavors Unlimited
A wide range of pre-prepared flavors are available in this ice cream parlor along the Russian River that's a customary stop on hot days. The owners will mix up gelatos and frozen yogurts to taste. Mix-in options include candies, nuts, and fruits. ✪ *16450 Main St., Guerneville, 95446 • Map G3 • 707 869 2927 • Open 8:30am–9:30pm Thu–Tue, until 10pm Sat*

Top 10 Local Foods

1 Poultry
Free-range chickens are raised around Petaluma, known as the "Egg Capital of the World."

2 Sonoma Leg of Lamb
Sonoma County is known for raising sheep on pastures free of synthetic fertilizers, herbicides, and pesticides.

3 Gravenstein Apples
This delicious apple, native to Denmark, is grown around Sebastopol.

4 Olives
Many wineries grow olives, which are used to produce artisanal gourmet olive oils.

5 Ice cream
Three Twins makes delicious organic ice creams using local goats' milk. ✪ *Oxbow Public Market, 610 1st. St., Napa, 94559*

6 Oysters
Fresh-caught oysters can be purchased at Drakes Bay Oyster Farm. ✪ *17171 Sir Francis Drake Blvd., Inverness, 94937 • Map H6 • 415 669 1149 • Open 8:30am–4:30pm*

7 Cheese
Many wineries and delis sell cheese, including estate-produced cheese from Spring Hill Cheese Company. ✪ *621 Western Av., Petaluma, 94952 • Map K5 • 707 762 3446*

8 Beer
Wine Country breweries have a stellar reputation for producing artisanal craft beers.

9 Herbs
Lavender is grown at wineries such as Tanuda Ridge, host to Lynn's Lavender and Herb Garden. ✪ *3335 Harrison Grade Rd., Sebastopol, 95472 • Map H4 • 707 874 1060*

10 Mushrooms
Many species of edible mushroom grow in Wine Country and thrive in winter.

Left **Hot rock massage, Meadowood** Right **Waiting room, Kenwood Inn & Spa**

Spas

Dr. Wilkinson's Hot Springs Resort

A Calistoga institution, this resort is best known for the mud immersions that "Doc" Wilkinson pioneered in 1952 using volcanic ash and mineralized hot springs water. "The Works" package treats clients to every service the spa has to offer *(see p14)*.

Silverado Resort & Spa

Spanning 16,000 sq ft (1,500 sq m), this Roman-inspired spa has 16 private treatment rooms, a full-service beauty salon, a world-class fitness center, plus an 82-ft (25-m) lap pool and outdoor whirlpools *(see p18)*.

Spa Solage

With 20,000 sq ft (1,858 sq m), Spa Solage has been named the top spa in the Americas. Fed by geothermal mineral waters, its Bathhouse has 14 treatment rooms. There is also a gym and a yoga studio.

◈ 755 Silverado Trail, Calistoga, 94515
• Map K2 • www.solagecalistoga.com

Fairmont Sonoma Mission Inn & Spa

A deluxe spa, Fairmont Sonoma has its own source of thermal mineral water, bubbling up from underground at 135° Fahrenheit (57° C). Surrounded by exquisitely manicured grounds, this spa boasts many amenities for relaxation and rejuvenation.
◈ 100 Boyes Blvd., Sonoma, 95476
• Map L5 • www.fairmont.com/sonoma

Kenwood Inn & Spa

Known for its innovative vinotherapy, this spa uses red wine extracts and Chardonnay and Riesling oils extracted from grape seeds in its treatments. Couples can relax in a two-person Jacuzzi tub with vineyard views before or after a "wine wrap." ◈ 10400 Sonoma Hwy., Kenwood, 95452 • Map K4 • www. kenwoodinn.com

Treatment rooms, Spa Solage

The Spa at Villagio

Parquet floors, natural field-stone walls, soothing fountains, cascading waterfalls, and serene reflecting pools combine in this 13,000-sq-ft (1,208 sq m) Tuscan-inspired property. Five private spa suites feature flat-screen TVs, sunken tubs, and sumptuous creature comforts.

Spa suite, Villagio Inn

§ 6481 Washington St., Yountville, 94599 • Map L4 • www.villagio.com

The Spa at Meadowood

This deluxe spa offers treatments using organic grape products. The Grape Seed Rejuvenation, an invigorating skin polish followed by a grape-seed-oil massage, is relaxing after a game of tennis or golf, or hiking the 5 mile (7 km) Meadowood Loop. § 900 Meadowood Ln., St. Helena, 94574 • Map L3 • www.meadowood.com

Calistoga Ranch

Featuring Japanese-inspired architecture, this spa has outdoor thermal soaking pools overlooking an oak-shaded creek. Treatments include sensual massages, lavish skin care, and a dry-brush body exfoliation followed by a mustard seed and seaweed body wrap. § 580 Lommel Rd., Calistoga, 94515 • Map K2 • www.calistogaranch.com

The Carneros Inn

Spa treatments are based on the use of local products and ingredients – from apricots, mustards, and olives to grapes and goat butter – in this chic spa. Its signature Huichica Creek thermal bath features a jet massage as a prelude to treatments. Private outdoor baths offer sweeping vistas of the wine district. § 4048 Sonoma Hwy., Napa, 94559 • Map L5 • www.thecarnerosinn.com

Osmosis Day Spa Sanctuary

Sign up for a rejuvenating Cedar Enzyme Bath at this day spa surrounded by vineyards. Clients steep in a bed of ground evergreens, and penetrating heat is generated biologically by fermentation. After the treatment, find inner peace in the Zen meditation garden (see p92).

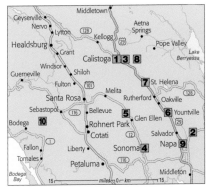

AROUND CALIFORNIA WINE COUNTRY

CALIFORNIA WINE COUNTRY'S TOP 10

Left **Main Street, St. Helena** Center **Corkscrew collection on display, CIA** Right **Oakville winery**

Napa Valley

EMMED BY FORESTED MOUNTAIN SLOPES, *this narrow valley extends north about 30 miles (48 km) from the town of Napa to Calistoga. Synonymous with wine production in California, Napa Valley draws maximum visitors to Wine Country thanks to its more than 300 wineries, natural and historic attractions, deluxe spas, exquisite country inns, and some eminent fine-dining restaurants. On warm summer weekends, Hwy. 29 is choked with stop-and-go-traffic. The valley is misty in winter, blossom-laden in spring, cloudless in summer, and enlivened by gold and crimson foliage in fall.*

Lush green vineyards, Napa Valley

🔟 Sights

1. The Napa Riverfront
2. Napa Valley Wine Train
3. The Hess Collection
4. Oakville
5. St. Helena
6. The Rhine House
7. Auberge du Soleil
8. Culinary Institute of America
9. Castello di Amorosa
10. Calistoga

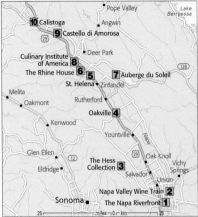

Preceding pages **Parducci Wine Cellars, Ukiah**

1 The Napa Riverfront

Spruced up after a multi-million dollar renovation, the historic Riverfront District bustles with commercial activity. The 10-block stretch along Main Street and the Napa River is anchored by the commanding red-brick

The Napa Riverfront

Hatt Building, hosting fine-dining restaurants, boutiques, and the chic Napa River Inn *(see p118)*, with rooms overlooking the river. A wetland rehabilitation plan has lured waterbirds. Napa River Adventures offers trips aboard canvas-topped, electric-driven gondolas. ◈ *Map P6*

2 Napa Valley Wine Train

A trip aboard the Napa Valley Wine Train *(see pp12–13)* is a romantic way to enjoy the scenery while savoring regional cuisine and wines. The 3-hour round-trip experience between Napa and St. Helena is enhanced by the elegance of the restored vintage carriages, which includes an elevated Vista Dome. Tour options include Napa Valley's only evening winery tour, with a special after-hours visit to Grgich Hills Estate winery *(see p71)*.

3 The Hess Collection

A long country lane leads up the slopes of Mount Veeder to this winery *(see pp8–9)*. Its contemporary art gallery displays only a fraction of owner Donald Hess's collection of more than 1,000 pieces by world-famous artists. Hess's Mount Veeder Cabernet Sauvignon can be tasted in the 1903 winery, which opens onto a courtyard garden.

4 Oakville

This quaint hamlet evolved in the 1870s as one of California's most important wine centers. Today considered one of the premier terroirs for Cabernet Sauvignon, the 2-mile (3-km) wide Oakville AVA extends across the valley and up the flanks of the Mayacamas Mountains to the west and the Vaca Mountains to the east. ◈ *Map L4*

Napa Valley Wine Train

American Indians

In pre-Columbian times, the Napa Valley was populated by three groups of American Indians: Patwin, Pomo, and Wappo. They lived well by hunting, fishing, and gathering. By the 1880s, these groups had been herded into missions or reservations, and many succumbed to smallpox and other diseases introduced by European settlers.

St. Helena

Known as the heart of Napa Valley, this peaceful town could serve as a model for a "Small Town, U.S.A" postcard. Its old-fashioned Main Street is lined with antique stores and restaurants, posh wine bars, and cafés spilling onto the sidewalks. St. Helena has many sites to visit, including the Silverado Museum *(see p45)*, Victorian Rhine House, and the Culinary Institute of America *(see pp16–17)*, and, outside town, the Bale Grist Mill *(see p52)*, and Bothe-Napa Valley State Park *(see p50)*. ✪ *Map L3*

The Rhine House

Fronted by fountains, this icon of the Beringer wine label rises over St. Helena. Completed in 1884, the ornate stone-and-timber, 17-room Victorian mansion was built for winery founder Frederick Beringer. Its gables, steep spires, and the 41 stained-glass windows all display fine craftsmanship. Listed on the National Register of Historic Places, it serves as the winery's tasting room. ✪ *2000 Main St., St. Helena, 94574 • Map L3 • 707 967 4412 • Open 10am–6pm summer, 10am–5pm winter • Adm • www.beringer.com*

Auberge du Soleil

Auberge du Soleil

Perched on the edge of the Vaca Mountains, this premium resort evokes visions of the French Riviera with its olive groves, terraced sandstone-colored villas, and sweeping views over vineyards below. Day-visitors are lured uphill to Auberge du Soleil's acclaimed spa for a lemon-olive oil massage and other treatments; and to the restaurant, where chef Robert Curry serves divine seasonal dishes. ✪ *180 Rutherford Hill Rd, Rutherford, 94573 • Map L3 • 707 963 1211 • www.aubergedusoleil.com*

Culinary Institute of America

Founded in 1946, The Culinary Institute of America *(see pp16–17)* offers degree-level tuition, plus short classes and demonstrations in culinary arts and wine studies. Its grandiose castle-like campus began life in 1889 as Greystone Cellars winery, and was the Christian Brothers winery from 1950 to 1990 under winemaker Brother Timothy. His vast corkscrew collection is on view in the mammoth

Stained glass, Rhine House

The Rhine House's stained-glass windows accounted for one-quarter of its $28,000 construction costs.

lobby. The Wine Spectator Restaurant serves delicious cuisine prepared by students, and hosts special tasting events.

Castello di Amorosa

The dream of vintner Dario Sattui, this mammoth structure has 107 rooms on eight levels and took 14 years to complete. Beyond its drawbridge and crenelated turrets and walls, the 121,000 sq-ft (11,200 sq-m) castle has a chapel, a frescoed hall, and a torture chamber with, among other things, an antique "iron maiden" torture device. The huge barrel cellar and tasting rooms are beneath the castle, which hosts a midsummer Medieval Festival with jousting (see p15).

Castello di Amorosa

Calistoga

This spa-resort town (see pp14–15) dates back to the 1880s when it was established on the site of hot springs, and a railroad was built to get visitors to partake of the thermal waters. Calistoga retains much of its original architecture: Lincoln Avenue, its main street, looks much as it did more than a century ago. Key sites include the old City Hall and train depot, the Old Faithful Geyser (see p14), Sterling Vineyards (see p15), and Clos Pegase (see p15). ◉ Map K2

A One-day Drive along Hwy. 29

Morning

🕐 Begin in downtown Napa and exit north on the St. Helena Hwy. 29, passing **Domaine Chandon** (see p71) on your left. After a stop to sample sparkling wines at this stylish winery, continue through **Yountville** (see p70) to Oakville, calling at **Oakville Grocery** (see p66) to peruse this world-class deli and perhaps buy items for a picnic lunch. Nearby, visit **Robert Mondavi Winery** (see p71), built in 1966 as the first major winery in Napa since Prohibition; factor in at least one hour for a fascinating and educational tour. Then, arriving at **V. Sattui Winery** (see p60), you'll want to picnic beneath the shady trees on the lush lawns.

Afternoon

Stroll through St. Helena before continuing north past **The Rhine House** (see p68). A short distance beyond, pull into the **Culinary Institute of America** (see pp16–17) to view the corkscrew collection and Vintners Hall of Fame, and perhaps even witness a cooking demonstration. Continue to **Bale Grist Mill** (see p52) to admire the old mill and giant water wheel, and to enjoy a walk amid the Douglas fir and redwood forest. After another 2 miles (4 km), a medieval-style castle – **Castello di Amorosa** (see p15) – on your left proves an irresistible temptation to visit: allow an hour here before continuing along Hwy. 29 to Calistoga. Turn right onto Lincoln Av. for the town center and the end of your drive.

Explore the Castello di Amorosa vineyards on horse-drawn carriage tours on weekends.

69

Left **Napa Valley Bike Tour** Right **Napa Valley Museum**

🔟 Best of the Rest

Main Street Napa

Historic buildings of note line Napa's Main Street and murals depicting scenes from local history adorn many walls. The 1880 Italianate Napa Valley Opera House is here. 🗺 *Map P6*

Yountville

The tiny, tree-lined town of Yountville is famous for its many quality restaurants. Winery and Napa Valley Museum *(see p45)* are the key sites here. 🗺 *Map L4*

Napa River

A multi-million dollar restoration program has brought this once polluted watercourse back to life with fish and birdlife. The Napa river is navigable from Napa city southward. 🗺 *Map M5*

Oxbow Public Market

A health-food lover's paradise, this airy market in downtown Napa has more than two dozen restaurants, cafés, and fresh food retailers. It also hosts a twice-weekly outdoor farmers' market. 🗺 *644 1st St. # D., Napa, 94559 • Map P5 • www. oxbowpublicmarket.com*

Bicycling

Running along the east side of Napa Valley, parallel to Hwy 29, the Silverado Trail is tailor-made for bicycling. Napa Valley Bike Tours rents bikes and offers tours. 🗺 *6795 Washington St., Yountville, 94599 • Map L4 • 707 251 8687 • www.napavalleybiketours.com*

St. Helena Olive Oil Company

In addition to extra virgin olive oil, this store sells an eclectic range of local products, including wine vinegars, herbs, mustards, and nut and seed oils, plus toiletries. 🗺 *1351 Main St., St. Helena, 94574 • Map L3 • http://sholiveoil.com*

First Presbyterian Church

With its soaring spire and steep gable, this clapboard church, built in 1874, is a superb example of late Victorian Gothic architecture. 🗺 *1333 3rd St., Napa, 94559 • Map P6 • 707 224 8693*

Napa Mill

This riverfront building was built in the mid-1800s and has served as a mill, warehouse, and skating rink. It hosts boutiques, restaurants, and a deluxe hotel. 🗺 *500 Main St., Napa, 94559 • Map P6 • 707 252 9372 • www.historicnapamill.com*

Ballooning

Flights begin with the roar of burners filling giant balloons with hot air, followed by silence as the crafts rise over the valley. 🗺 *301 Post St., Napa, 94559 • 707 944 0228 • www.napavalleyballoons.com*

Skyline Wilderness Park

The 6-mile (10-km) loop trail through this park passes through meadows and California oak forest. You can spot coyotes and wild turkeys here. 🗺 *2201 Imola Av., Napa, 94559 • Map M5 • www. skylinepark.org*

The Silverado Trail is named for the wagons that hauled silver from the cinnabar mines on Mount St. Helena in the 19th century.

Left **Domaine Chandon** Center **Barrel room, The Hess Collection** Right **Robert Mondavi Winery**

Napa Valley Wineries

Domaine Chandon
Owned by France's Moët-Hennessy champagne house, this winery has a tasting room and a leafy terrace graced by contemporary sculptures. Tours are offered. ✪ *1 California Dr., Yountville, 94599 • Map L4 • 707 944 2892*

Stag's Leap Winery
A family-run winery, Stag's Leap is world-renowned for its Cabernet Sauvignon. Appointment-only tours include the barrel cave, with 17th-century celestial maps *(see pp18–19)*.

Beaulieu Vineyard
This century-old, imposing, natural stone winery rises over Hwy 29. Choose from tastings of BV's distinctive Cabernets to an appointment-only tour. ✪ *1960 St. Helena Hwy., Rutherford, 94573 • Map L3 • www.bvwines.com*

The Hess Collection
The wines – especially the estate-produced Mount Veeder labels – are reason enough to visit, but the main draw is the art collection *(see pp8–11)*.

Frog's Leap Winery
Occupying an old red barn and modern tasting room, Frog's Leap is a fun-focused winery. Its free tours highlight the winery's organic practices and end with tastings of its Sauvignon Blanc. ✪ *8815 Conn Creek Rd., Rutherford, 94573 • Map L3 • www.frogsleap.com*

Grgich Hills Estate
The wines from this winery have been served to Presidents Reagan and Clinton, Queen Elizabeth II, and French President François Mitterrand. ✪ *1829 St. Helena Hwy., Rutherford, 94573 • Map L3 • www.grgich.com*

Inglenook
Formerly known as Rubicon estate, this winery is owned by Francis Ford Coppola. The iconic ivy-clad chateau was completed in 1891 and houses a museum. ✪ *1991 St. Helena Hwy., Rutherford, 94573 • Map L3 • www.rubiconestate.com*

Opus One
This winery is dedicated to producing its acclaimed Opus One Cabernet Sauvignon blend. Its minimalist structure is furnished with European antiques. ✪ *7900 St. Helena Hwy., Oakville, 94562 • Map L4 • www.opusonewinery.com*

Plumpjack Winery
Situated at the base of the Vaca Mountain range, this Oakville AVA winery is acclaimed for its limited production, estate Cabernet Sauvignons. ✪ *620 Oakville Cross Rd., Oakville, 94562 • Map L3 • www.plumpjack.com*

Robert Mondavi Winery
A distinctive archway and bell tower greet visitors at this winery, which reflects early Mission architecture. ✪ *7801 Hwy. 29, Oakville, 94562 • Map L3 • www.robertmondavi.com*

Robert Mondavi partnered with French vintner Baron Philippe de Rothschild to create Opus One in 1980.

Left **Art gallery, Mumm Napa** Right **Old red tractor at Tudal Winery**

ɪ0 Unique Wineries

Clos Pegase Winery
Look for contemporary art pieces by Wassily Kandinsky and Max Ernst, and Henry Moore's *Gaia* at the entrance of this Cretan-inspired Post-Modernist winery (see pp14–15).

Fontanella Family Vineyard
Members of the wine club can order wine with their own name on the labels here. A case discount is offered on joining, too. ◈ 1721 Partrick Rd., Napa, 94558 • Map M5 • www.fontanellawinery.com

Mumm Napa
Featuring an art gallery with a permanent display of original photographs by Ansel Adams, this winery produces sparkling wines. ◈ 8445 Silverado Trail, Rutherford, 94573 • Map L3 • 707 967 7770 • Open 10am–4:45pm • Adm • www.mummnapa.com

Sterling Vineyards
A stunning hilltop perch, great architecture, and a fascinating tour are reasons to visit, but the big draw is the aerial tram ride that whisks visitors 300 ft (91 m) to the winery (see pp14–15).

Kuleto Estate
Kuleto's tasting room – the Tuscan-style Villa Cusina – has a fantastic view of Lake Hennessey and the Napa Valley from its mountain setting. It is entered by use of a secret gate code. ◈ 2470 Sage Canyon Rd., St. Helena, 94574 • Map L3 • www.kuletoestate.com

Darioush
Iranian owner Shahpar Khaledi built this winery in the style of a Persian palace, with water features and freestanding sandstone columns topped by horses (see pp18–19).

Artesa Winery
Architect Domingo Triay designed Artesa with a grass-covered roof. It has an artist-in-residence, art, and sculptures throughout, and striking water features. ◈ 1345 Henry Rd., Napa, 94559 • Map L5 • www.artesawinery.com

Castello di Amorosa
A fantasy in stone, this re-creation of an Italian castle measures 121,000 sq ft (1,124 sq m), is entered by a drawbridge, and features turrets and dungeons stocked with torture instruments (see pp14–15).

Far Niente
Former race-car driver and winery owner Gil Nickel has stocked the Carriage House with classic cars, including his own race cars. ◈ 1350 Acacia Dr., Oakville, 94562 • Map L4 • www.farniente.com

Tudal Winery
This small winery names its Tractor Shed Red for an antique red tractor standing outside an old shed. Vintage tractors and farming implements are scattered about the vineyard. ◈ 1015 Big Tree Rd., St. Helena, 94574 • Map L3 • www.tudalwinery.com

Left **V. Sattui Winery** Right **Entrance, Oakville Grocery**

10 Places to Shop

1 Oakville Grocery
Advertised by a vintage Coca-Cola sign, this grocery has served the Napa Valley community for more than 120 years.
⌀ *7856 St. Helena Hwy., Oakville, 94562* • Map L4 • www.oakvillegrocery.com

2 V. Sattui Winery
An ivy-clad winery with a huge delicatessen stocked with hundreds of types of cheeses, salamis, pâtés, olives, and breads. Sattui's wines are sold only here.
⌀ *1111 White Ln., St. Helena, 94574* • Map L3 • 707 963 7774 • www.vsattui.com

3 Taste Gallery
On the Michael Mondavi Family Estate, this wine studio sells wines from seven Mondavi family wineries throughout Northern California. Limited production wines available.
⌀ *1285 Dealy Ln., Napa, 94559* • Map L5 • www.michaelmondavifamilyestate.com

4 Napa Premium Outlets
There are numerous discount stores and boutiques, including top designer brands in this shopping center. ⌀ *629 Factory Stores Dr., Napa, 94559* • Map M5 • www. premium outlets.com/outlets/outlet.asp?id=25

5 Mill Street Antiques
Some 30 antique dealers have stores in this plaza totaling more than 10,000 sq ft (930 sq m) of floor space. You can spend hours here searching for that hidden gem.
⌀ *44 Mill St., Healdsburg, 95448* • Map H2 • 707 433 8409 • Open 11am–5pm

6 Oxbow Public Market
This spacious modern market is the go-to place for fresh produce, fish or meats, artisanal cheeses, rare wines, or other goodies for a picnic *(see p70)*.

7 JV Wine
Wines from around the world are available here at discount prices, plus there's an impressive choice of artisanal beers. The tasting bar hosts special tastings. ⌀ *301 1st St., Napa, 94559* • Map M5 • www.jvwine.com

8 Napa General Store
A riverfront store selling an eclectic range of local products, from art and artisanal jewelry to furniture and kitchen items made from wine barrels. ⌀ *540 Main St., Napa, 94559* • Map M5 • www. napageneralstore.com

9 V Marketplace
This assembly of specialty shops and restaurants includes a wine cellar and tasting room within and around the 141 year-old cobblestoned Groezinger Winery complex. ⌀ *6525 Washington St., Yountville, 94599* • Map L4 • www.vmarketplace.com

10 Woodhouse Chocolate
Housed in a charming 19th-century store, this family-run business sells decadent handmade chocolates. Hot chocolate in seven flavors is a highlight.
⌀ *1367 Main St., St. Helena, 94574* • Map L3 • www.woodhousechocolate.com

Left **Café Sarafornia** Right **Carpe Diem**

Bars, Cafés, and Clubs

The White Barn

A former winery carriage house, the White Barn hosts an eclectic annual calendar that includes every music type from country to jazz. *2727 Sulphur Springs Av., St. Helena, 94574 • Map L3 • 707 251 8715*

Downtown Joe's

This downtown Napa institution serves six artisanal brews year-round, as well as seasonal beers. It also hosts live music. *902 Main St., Napa, 94559 • Map P5 • 707 258 2337 • Open 8am–midnight daily*

Napa Valley Brewing Company

Hosted at the Calistoga Inn, this small brewpub stocks Calistoga Wheat Ale, Pilsner, Red Ale and Porter, plus seasonal brews. *1250 Lincoln Av., Calistoga, 94515 • Map K2 • 707 942 4101 • Open 11:30am–midnight daily*

Silo's

Live music is played in this music lounge with wine bar on Thursday, Friday, and Saturday nights. *530 Main St. C. Napa, 94559 • Map L3 • 707 251 5833*

Napa Valley Coffee Roasting Company

This cozy coffee shop roasts its own gourmet cafés. Its baristas brew delicious coffee at the espresso bar. *948 Main St., Napa, 94559 • Map P5 • 707 224 2233 • Open 7am–7pm daily*

Café Sarafornia

In the heart of Calistoga, this café-diner is a great breakfast spot. The lunch menu includes charbroiled salmon fillet. *1413 Lincoln Av., Calistoga, 94515 • Map K2 • 707 942 0555 • Open 7am–2:30pm • $$*

Bistro Don Giovanni

Chef Donna Scala serves gourmet Mediterranean fare at this downtown Napa bistro. *4110 Howard Ln., Napa, 94558 • Map M5 • 707 224 3300 • Open 11:30am–10pm Sun–Thur, 11:30am–11pm Fri & Sat • $$$$*

Uva Trattoria

Serving delicious Italian fare, Uva Trattoria hosts live blues, jazz, pop, and rock music five nights a week. *1040 Clinton St., Napa, 94559 • Map M5 • 707 255 6646 • Open 11:30am–9pm Sun–Thu, 11:30am–9:30pm Fri & Sat • $$$*

Silverado Brewing Company

Housed in the Freemark Abbey Winery building, the Silverado Brewing Company offers a five-course Brewer's Dinner. *3020 N. St. Helena Hwy., St. Helena, 94574 • Map L3 • 707 967 9876 • Open 11:30am–8:30pm Mon–Thu, 11:30am–9pm Fri–Sat, 11:30am–8:30pm Sun • $$*

Carpe Diem

Many unknown labels, plus local artisanal brews, are stocked in this hip wine bar. *1001 2nd St., Napa, 94559 • 707 224 0800 • Open 4–10pm Sun–Thu, 4–11pm Fri & Sat • $$*

Price Categories

For a three-course meal for one with half a bottle of wine (or equivalent meal), taxes and extra charges.	**$** under $20
	$$ $20–$40
	$$$ $40–$55
	$$$$ $55–$80
	$$$$$ over $80

Left **Mustards Grill**

Restaurants

Celadon
Situated in the Napa Mill, Celadon fuses Asian influences with local ingredients. ⚅ *500 Main St., Suite G., Napa, 94559 • Map P6 • 707 254 9690 • Open 11:30am–9pm Mon–Fri, 5–9pm Sat & Sun • $$$$*

The French Laundry
French-inspired dishes are the specialty at this world-renowned restaurant. ⚅ *6440 Washington St., Yountville, 94599 • Map L4 • 707 944 2380 • Open 11am–1pm Fri–Sun, 5:30–9:15pm daily • $$$$$*

Mustards Grill
Regional American dishes with global influences are served here. ⚅ *7399 St. Helena Hwy., Napa, 94558 • Map L3 • 707 944 2424 • Open 11:30am–9pm Mon–Thu, 11:30am–10pm Fri, 11am–10pm Sat, 11am–9pm Sun • $$*

Rutherford Grill
The meat-centric menu in this restaurant delights carnivores. ⚅ *1180 Rutherford Rd., Rutherford, 94573 • Map L3 • 707 963 1792 • Open 11:30am–9:30pm Sun–Thu, 11:30am–10:30pm Fri & Sat • $$$*

Étoile
This fine-dining restaurant is located in the Domaine Chandon winery *(see p71)*. Dishes are paired to the winery's champagnes. ⚅ *Open 11:30am–2:30pm, 6–9pm Thu–Mon • $$$$$*

ZuZu
A local favorite, cozy ZuZu offers bargain-priced mouth-sized treats. ⚅ *829 Main St., Napa, 94559 • Map P6 • 707 224 8555 • Open 11:30am–2:30pm & 4:30–10pm Mon–Fri (to 11pm Fri), 4:30–11pm Sat, 4:30–9:30pm Sun • $$$*

Brannan's Grill
Exuding old-world richness, Brannan's Grill offers nouvelle Californian cuisine. ⚅ *1374 Lincoln Av., Calistoga, 94515 • Map K2 • 707 942 2233 • Open 11:30am–10pm daily (from 11am Sat & Sun) • $$$*

Hurley's
This Mediterranean restaurant offers a prix fixe lunch, plus a late night bar menu. ⚅ *6518 Washington St., Yountville, 94599 • Map L4 • 707 944 2345 • Open 11:30am–10pm daily • $$$*

Bouchon
A casual bistro, Bouchon offers fare such as French onion soup and quiches. ⚅ *6534 Washington St., Yountville, 94599 • Map L4 • 707 944 8037 • Open 11:30am–midnight daily • $$$$*

Angèle
Nouvelle French-California dishes using local ingredients highlight the menu. ⚅ *540 Main St., Napa, 94559 • Map P6 • 707 252 8115 • Open 11:30am–9pm Sun–Thu, 11:30am–10pm Fri & Sat • $$$$*

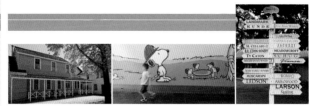

Left **Sonoma State Historic Park** Center **Charles M. Schulz Museum** Right **Glen Ellen**

Sonoma Valley and Santa Rosa

SEPARATED FROM NAPA VALLEY by the Mayacamas Mountains, with the Sonoma Mountain range to the west, this scenic vale was the birth-place of California's wine industry. At its southern end, the picturesque town of Sonoma is graced by carefully preserved historic buildings anchored by Sonoma Plaza, including the last of the 21 Spanish missions built in California by Franciscan padres. On the other hand, Santa Rosa, at the north end of the valley, has the Railroad District preserving 19th-century buildings that survived the 1906 earthquake. Many of Wine Country's most intriguing museums are here, too. And the region is strewn with areas perfect for outdoor activities.

Railroad Square District

🔟 Sights

1. Sonoma State Historic Park
2. Sonoma Plaza
3. Charles M. Schulz Museum
4. Railroad Square Historic District
5. Luther Burbank Home & Gardens
6. Jack London State Historic Park
7. Chateau St. Jean
8. Glen Ellen
9. Gloria Ferrer Caves & Vineyards
10. Sonoma County Museum

Valley of the Moon Winery, Glen Ellen

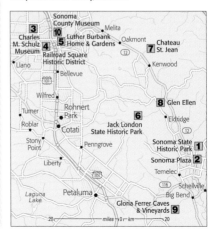

Sonoma Plaza was the birthplace of the California State Bear Flag, created during the 1846 Bear Flag Revolt.

1 Sonoma State Historic Park

This park preserves the Wine Country's foremost historic ensemble *(see pp20–21)*. The buildings here include the Spanish mission founded in 1823, and several Mexican-style adobe structures associated with the city's formative years when it was the political center of Northern California. General Mariano Vallejo's Gothic Revival house – Lachryma Montis *(see pp22–3)* – is an unmissable attraction. It stands at the end of a tree-lined driveway and is surrounded on three sides by natural meadows comprising two-thirds of the park.

Sonoma State Historic Park

2 Sonoma Plaza

El Pueblo de Sonoma was laid out around an 8-acre (3-ha) plaza that originally served as a parade ground. Still ringed by historic buildings, today it is a National Historic Landmark, has lawns shaded by trees, and serves as the town's focal point, notably during the Farmers' Market every Tuesday evening April through October. The City Hall at its heart was built of basalt stone in 1908 and has four identical sides. The Sonoma Valley Visitors Bureau is in the southeast quadrant *(see p20)*.

Sonoma Plaza

3 Charles M. Schulz Museum

Fascinating exhibits relating to the life of cartoonist Charles M. Schulz are on display here. Original drawings of the *Peanuts* cartoon strip provide hours of chuckles. Upstairs exhibits track Schulz's life, including his days in the army during WW II, when he illustrated his diaries and letters. His studio is re-created here. The museum also screens cartoon videos. Adults and kids alike can learn about cartooning, draw their own, and view them on a zoetrope in the Education Room *(see p24)*. ✎ www.schulzmuseum.org

4 Railroad Square Historic District

In the late-19th century, Santa Rosa thrived as the agricultural hub of the region, and Railroad Square was the heart of downtown. Hundreds of Italian families settled here, and Italian stone masons built the impressive basalt buildings that still grace the square today. Restoration in recent decades turned former canneries, warehouses, and food-processing plants into bars, restaurants, and specialty shops, all lent yesteryear ambience by their exposed brick walls and cast-iron features. The California Welcome Center and Santa Rosa Convention and Visitors Bureau are here *(see p25)*. ✎ http:// railroadsquare.net

The Sonoma Valley Visitors Bureau has brochures, maps, and a "2-for-1" booklet with wine-tasting coupons.

77

Luther Burbank

Born in Lancaster, Massachusetts, Luther Burbank (1849–1926) grew up on a farm and evolved a life-long fascination for botany. He purchased a 4-acre (1.6-ha) plot of land in Santa Rosa, where he developed hundreds of new varieties of fruits, plants, and flowers, including a spineless cactus and the Russet potato.

Luther Burbank Home & Gardens

5 Luther Burbank Home & Gardens

The former home, greenhouse, and gardens of world-renowned horticulturist Luther Burbank are a stellar Santa Rosa attraction. This unique city park preserves his spacious clapboard Greek Revival house, topped by a cupola and furnished with period pieces. The Carriage House Gift Shop and Museum tells the story of Burbank's experiments with plants during his 50-year career. The gardens have speciality sections, and burst with color in every season. Burbank is buried near the greenhouse (see p24).

6 Jack London State Historic Park

Adventurer and author Jack London built his home at this woodsy site in 1905 and lived here until his death in 1916. More than 10 miles (16 km) of trails lace the 1,400-acre (567-ha) park. Visitors can explore London's residence and studio, his vineyard and orchard, plus the lakeside bathhouse, and "The House of Happy Walls," which contains a museum. One trail leads to the ruins of "Wolf House," and to London's grave. ⌖ 2400 London Ranch Rd., Glen Ellen, 95442 • Map K4 • 707 938 5216 • Open 9:30am–5pm daily (Dec–Feb: closed Tue & Wed) • Adm • www.jacklondonpark.org

7 Chateau St. Jean

This winery, at the foot of Sugarloaf Ridge, has a typically Mediterranean feel to it. The chateau was built in the 1920s as a summer home for a mining magnate and is set amid gardens studded with classical statues. A statue of Jean, the winery's name-sake, welcomes guests in the main courtyard garden, graced by a decorative fountain. The winery is known for its white wines and consistent quality. ⌖ 8555 Sonoma Hwy., Kenwood, 95452 • Map K4 • 877 478 5326 • Open 10am–5pm • Adm • www.chateaustjean.com

8 Glen Ellen

A charming and quiet town, Glen Ellen is located in the heart of Sonoma Valley. The town evolved around the Glen Ellen Winery, founded in 1859 by Charles V. Stuart. Author Jack

Quarryhill Botanical Garden, Glen Ellen

London built his Beauty Ranch – today Jack London State Historic Park – in the hills west of town. The Quarryhill Botanical Garden delights with its collection of Asian plants. ◈ *Quarryhill Botanic Garden • Map K4 • 707 996 3166 • Open 9am–4pm • Adm • www.quarryhillbg.org*

Gloria Ferrer Vineyards

Gloria Ferrer Caves & Vineyards

Owned by Spanish sparkling wine giant, Freixenet, Gloria Ferrer's visitors center is styled as a Spanish farmhouse. A terrace offers sweeping views over the estate's olive groves and vineyards. Guided tours take in the long, cool cellars carved into the hillside. Award-winning extra-virgin olive oil is made here and sold in the gift shop. ◈ *23555 Carneros Hwy., Sonoma, 95476 • Map K5 • 707 933 1917 • Open 10am–5pm • Adm*

Sonoma County Museum

A 25,000-piece collection of documents, artwork, and artifacts relating to Sonoma County region's art, culture, and history is housed in this museum. There are also revolving exhibits of international scope, such as recent displays of Cuban art and the history of Communism in Sonoma County. The museum is located in the city's former main post office – a handsome Roman Renaissance Revival-style building built in 1909 (see p24). ◈ *Open 11am–5pm Tue–Sun • www.sonomacountymuseum.org*

A Walking Tour of Sonoma

Morning

Start your day at the visitor center at **Lachryma Montis** (see pp22–3). After exploring the various sites at General Vallejo's home, walk south along the tree-lined driveway and turn left onto the walking path that leads east through a broad meadow to Depot Park. This old train station is a museum dedicated to the town's history. Next, walk south through the parking lot to visit **La Casa Grande** and, east along Spain St., the **Toscano Hotel** and **Sonoma Barracks** (see pp20–21), headquarters of the Mexican army of the north frontier. Cross 1st St. E. to visit the **Mission San Francisco Solano de Sonoma** and the **Blue Wing Inn** (see pp20–21).

Afternoon

After lunch at one of the restaurants on the north-east corner of **Sonoma Plaza**, stroll through the square to admire the **Bear Flag Monument**, in the northeast, and **City Hall**, at its core (see pp20–21). Next, walk south down 1st St. E., past the **Sebastiani Theater** (see p80). Turn right onto Napa St., then left onto Broadway for the **Sonoma Valley Museum of Art** (see p80), on your right. Continue down Broadway past the **Hopmonk Tavern** (see p84) to France St. Turn right, then right onto 1st St. W. to return to **Sonoma Plaza**. Turn left onto Spain St. After half a mile (400 m), **Lachryma Montis** is signed at 3rd St. W. Turn right to return to the visitor center.

Left **Sebastiani Theatre** Center **Prince Memorial Greenway** Right **The Civic Artwalk**

🔟 Best of the Rest

1 Church of One Tree
Reopened in 2011 after a restoration program, this church *(see p25)* was made from the lumber of a single redwood tree that stood 275 ft (83.8 m) tall and had a diameter of 18 ft (5.5 m).

2 Sonoma Valley Museum of Art
Exhibiting works by local and international artists, such as British artist David Hockney, this museum spans the spectrum from painting to film. ◈ *551 Broadway, 95476 • Map L5 • www.svma.org*

3 Safari West
Bring the kids to make the most of this African-themed safari park. Visitors tour in open-top vehicles, guaranteeing close-up viewing of giraffes, rhinos, and leopards *(see p25)*.

4 Shiloh Ranch Regional Park
A hilly retreat spanning 850 acres (345 ha), this park is laced with trails for hiking, cycling and horse-back riding. One trail leads to the top of Shiloh Ridge, where a picnic area offers views *(see p25)*.

5 Prince Memorial Greenway
This formerly deteriorated urban creek running through downtown Santa Rosa has been revived, and draws marsh birds, waterfowl, and fish. A bicycle and pedestrian path links downtown and Railroad Square *(see p25)*.

6 The Civic Artwalk
Downtown Santa Rosa is studded with contemporary sculptures of every size, shape, and form. The walk begins at Depot Square and takes in 38 pieces strewn along the thorough-fares and plazas *(see p25)*.

7 Sugarloaf Ridge State Park
This mountain retreat has trails that reach atop Bald Mountain (2,729 ft/832 m), from where the Sierra Nevada can be seen. ◈ *2605 Adobe Canyon Rd., Kenwood, 95452 • Map L4 • 707 833 5712*

8 Petaluma River Cruise
A journey downriver from the turning basin in downtown Petaluma to San Pablo Bay grants a different perspective on Wine Country. ◈ *Dolphin Charters, 1007 Leneve Place El Cerrito, 94530 • www.dolphincharters.com*

9 Sebastiani Theatre
Built in 1933 by vintner Samuele Sebastiani, this theater was designed in Italian Renaissance style by architect James W. Reid. ◈ *476 1st St. E., Sonoma, 95476 • Map L5*

10 Pacific Coast Air Museum
This museum delights aviation and military history enthusiasts with its collection of fighter jets and other aircraft, from an F-14 Tomcat to an Albatross seaplane. ◈ *2230 Becker Blvd., Santa Rosa, 95403 • Map J3 • 707 575 7900 • Open 10am–4pm Tue, Thu, Sat & Sun*

Left **Tasting room, Valley of the Moon Winery** Right **Sebastiani Vineyards**

Wineries

Sebastiani Vineyards
This winery was founded in 1904 by Italian immigrant Samuele Sebastiani. Tours include old wine-making equipment, and a trolley leads through old vineyards. ⬡ *389 4th St. E., Sonoma, 95476 • Map L5 • www.sebastiani.com*

Kenwood Vineyards
More than 14,000 oak barrels fill this hillside winery. Its tasting room is in the original 1906 wooden barn-like structure.
⬡ *9592 Sonoma Hwy., 95452 • Map K4*
• www.kenwoodvineyards.com

Kunde Estate Winery
Sprawling over 2,000 acres (810 ha), Kunde Estate is still in family hands more than a century after its founding. It offers free tours of the barrel caves, plus mountaintop tastings.
⬡ *9825 Sonoma Hwy., Kenwood, 95452*
• Map K4 • www.kunde.com

Ravenswood Winery
Wine tasting is made a fun experience here, to be enjoyed in a rustic old stone winery with patios, gardens, and picnic areas.
⬡ *18701 Gehricke Rd., Sonoma, 95476*
• Map L5 • www.ravenswoodwinery.com

Buena Vista Winery
Claiming to be the region's first winery, Buena Vista is on the site of Agoston Haraszthy's winery *(see p34)* established in 1858. Many old buildings still stand.
⬡ *18000 Old Winery Rd., Sonoma, 95476*
• Map L5 • http://buenavistacarneros.com

Benziger Winery
A visit to this rustic winery is a lesson in "biodynamic" farming. The tractor-drawn tour includes the barrel cave. ⬡ *1883 London Ranch Rd., Glen Ellen, 95442*
• Map K4 • www.benziger.com

Valley of the Moon Winery
Dating back to 1863, this winery has picnic areas and hosts special events, such as "Murder Mystery" dinners. ⬡ *777 Madrone Rd., Glen Ellen, 95442 • Map K4*
• www.valleyofthemoonwinery.com

Ledson Winery and Vineyards
Called "The Castle" by locals, this Gothic winery has six tasting bars. Its entire wine stock sells on site and to club members.
⬡ *7335 Sonoma Hwy., Kenwood, 95409*
• Map K4 • www.ledson.com

St. Francis Winery and Vineyards
Named for the Franciscan monks who planted the first vines in California, this mission-style winery produces red wines.
⬡ *100 Pythian Rd., Santa Rosa, 95409*
• Map J3 • www.stfranciswine.com

Bartholomew Park Winery
Its museum of Wine Country and wine-making history, formal garden, plus a replica of Agoston Haraszthy's Romanesque home add a unique charm to this boutique, limited-production winery. ⬡ *1000 Vineyard Ln., Sonoma, 95476 • Map L5 • www.bartpark.com*

Left **Miniature models, Cline Cellars** Center **B. R. Cohn Winery labels** Right **Matanzas Creek**

Wineries with Unique Attractions

Chateau St. Jean
Palatial Italianate architecture and sectional formal gardens with parterres separated by clipped privet hedges are the chief attractions of this winery *(see p78)*.

Kendall-Jackson Wine Center & Gardens
This winery's impressive gardens have separate parterres devoted to vegetable, herb, and edible flowers. The highlights are the red and white wine sensory gardens *(see p25)*.

Gundlach-Bundschu Winery
Making good use of its outdoor amphitheater, this winery hosts events such as the Huichica Music Festival, a Midsummer Mozart Festival, and a Summer Film Fest. ◈ *2000 Denmark St., Sonoma, 95476 • Map L5 • www.gunbun.com*

Cline Cellars
The California Missions Museum next to the tasting room here displays miniatures of the 21 California missions, made for the 1939 World's Fair in San Francisco. ◈ *24737 Arnold Dr., Sonoma, 95476 • Map L5 • www.clinecellars.com*

B. R. Cohn Winery
An underground geothermal aquifer warms the B.R. Cohn terroire. Also unique is the owner's hot-rod collection, reflected on the labels of his wines. ◈ *15000 Sonoma Hwy., Glen Ellen, 95442 • Map K4 • www.brcohn.com*

Imagery Estate Winery
Examine the world's largest collection of wine label art at this boutique winery. Every year the winery commissions new art for each vintage. ◈ *14335 Sonoma Hwy., Glen Ellen, 95442 • Map K4 • www.imagerywinery.com*

Matanzas Creek Winery
Visit this winery in late spring, when its lavender fields are in purple bloom and the air is redolent with scent. ◈ *6097 Bennett Valley Rd., Santa Rosa, 95404 • Map K4 • www.matanzascreek.com*

Kaz Vineyard
Named for owner Richard Kasmier, this winery produces experimental wines using rare grape varietals, such as Alicante, Counoise, and Lenoir. ◈ *233 Adobe Canyon Rd., Kenwood, 95452 • Map K4 • www.kazwinery.com*

Jacuzzi Family Winery
Step into the Tuscan winery to sample Italian-style wines, plus artisanal olive oils. The family invented the Jacuzzi hydrotherapy bathtub. ◈ *24724 Arnold Dr., Sonoma, 95476 • Map L5 • www.jacuzziwines.com*

Viansa Winery
This winery overlooks the Carneros wetlands. More than one million birds flock here in winter and spring. Bring your binoculars. ◈ *25200 Arnold Dr., Sonoma, 95476 • Map L5 • www.viansa.com*

Left **Benziger Biodynamic Vineyard tram tour** Right **Cheetah, Safari West**

Children's Attractions

Safari West
Children will love an open-top safari through the park's savanna-like chaparral, stocked with giraffe, rhino, and other African creatures *(see p25)*.

Train Town
Take a ride on a quarter-scale 1875 Baldwin Mogul steam train around a 1.5-mile (2.5-km) track lined with quarter-scale 19th-century buildings. ◈ *20264 Broadway, Sonoma, 95476 • Map L5 • www.traintown.com*

Robert Ferguson Observatory
Visitors can view the skies day or night through a 6.6-ft (2-m) refractor telescope in this observatory inside Sugarloaf Ridge State Park *(see p80)*. ◈ *http://rfo.org*

Plaza Duck Pond, Sonoma
Geese and mallards paddle around this reed-fringed duck pond on the southwest corner of Sonoma Plaza. An adjacent playground provides further fun. ◈ *Sonoma Plaza, Spain St. between 2nd & 4th, Sonoma, 95476 • Map L5*

Horse Riding at Triple Creek
Guided horseback trips on the 1,850-acre (749-ha) Kunde ranch lead through vineyards, oak woodlands, and pastures. Riders get to enjoy views from atop the Mayacamas Mountains. ◈ *2400 London Ranch Rd., Glen Ellen, 95442 • www.triplecreekhorseoutfit.com*

MacDougald Skate Park
The largest skate park in Sonoma County is a highlight of 85-acre (35-ha) Maxwell Farms Regional Park. ◈ *Maxfield Farms Regional Park, 100 Verano Av., Sonoma, 95476 • Map L5 • 707 938 2794*

Benziger Biodynamic Vineyard Tram Tour
Tractor-pulled tram tours of the vineyards are offered, where children and adults get to learn about organic and sustainable farming methods *(see p81)*.

Snoopy's Gallery & Gift Shop
Across the street from the Charles M. Schulz Museum, this gift shop features over 15,000 *Peanuts*-related collectibles. It is part of Snoopy's Home ice rink. ◈ *www.snoopyshomeice.com*

Charles M. Schulz Museum
Fun and educational for the entire family, this museum displays hundreds of original *Peanuts* cartoons *(see p24)*.

Children's Museum of Sonoma County
Designed to stimulate children's curiosity in art, nature, and science, this museum opened in 2005. Its new home in a building next to the Charles M. Schulz Museum is awaiting completion in 2013 and is open on a limited basis. ◈ *1833 West Steele Ln., Santa Rosa, 95403 • Map J3 • http://cmosc.org*

Left **Cellars of Sonoma** Center **Murphy's Irish Pub** Right **Centre du Vin**

🔟 Bars, Cafés, and Clubs

1 Centre du Vin
A chic lounge bar in the Ledson Hotel, Centre du Vin has classic French bistro décor, and indoor-outdoor seating. ⊗ *480 1st St. E., Sonoma, 95476 • Map L5 • 707 996 9779 • Open 11:30am–midnight • www.centreduvin.com*

2 Murphy's Irish Pub
A great place to enjoy a pint, and pub food, Murphy's hosts literary events and live music. ⊗ *464 1st St. E., Sonoma, 95476 • Map L5 • 707 935 0660 • Open 11am–11pm Sun–Thu, 11am–midnight Fri & Sat*

3 Chrome Lotus
This nightclub has a 40-ft (12-m) long granite bar and large-screen TVs, and the Pool Lounge has billiards tables. ⊗ *501 Mendocino, Santa Rosa, 95404 • Map P1 •707843 5643 • Open 7pm–2am Mon–Thu, 5pm–2am Fri–Sat*

4 Last Day Saloon
Known for its excellent live music and comedy acts, the Last Day Saloon serves a full dinner menu. ⊗ *120 5th St., Santa Rosa, 95401 • Map N2 • 707 545 5876 • Open 4pm–midnight Wed & Thu, 4pm–2am Fri & Sat*

5 Russian River Brewing Company
This brewpub in downtown Santa Rosa offers a full line up of ales and lagers. The pub also hosts live music. ⊗ *725 4th St., Santa Rosa, 95404 • Map Q1 • 707 545 2337 • Open 11am–midnight Sun–Thu, 11am–1am Fri & Sat*

6 Sweetspot Pub & Lounge
Serving its own Lagunitas labels plus international draft beers, this English-style pub offers typical pub food. ⊗ *619 4th St., Santa Rosa, 95404 • Map P1 • 707 528 7566 • Open 2pm–midnight Mon–Thu, noon–midnight Fri–Sat, 10am–9pm Sun*

7 Hopmonk Tavern
Located in a renovated farmhouse, this stylish pub is popular with locals and visitors seeking good beer and beer-compatible cuisine. ⊗ *691 Broadway, Sonoma, 95476 • Map L5 • 707 935 9100 • Open 11:30am–9pm Mon–Sat (to 10pm Fri & Sat)*

8 Mystic Theater
The Mystic Theater was built in 1911 to host Vaudeville acts. Today the renovated theater is considered one of the Bay Area's premier live music venues. ⊗ *23 Petaluma Blvd. N., Petaluma, 94952 • Map K5 • 707 765 9211*

9 Steiner's Tavern
On the town plaza, this bar caters to beer-loving folks who prefer Budweiser and Coors to heartier artisanal brews. ⊗ *465 1st St. W., Sonoma, 95476 • Map L5 • 707 996 3812 • Open 6am–2am daily*

10 Cellars of Sonoma
Sample and buy rare, small-production new world wines in this tasting room in Railroad Square. ⊗ *133 4th St., Santa Rosa, 95401 • Map N2 • 707 578 1826 • Open 11am–8:30pm Tue & Wed, 11am–10:30pm Thu–Sat (to 10pm Fri), noon–8pm Sun*

Left **Della Santina's**

⭐10 Restaurants

1 Della Santina's
Patrons are assured the best of traditional Italian fare at Della Santina's. ◊ *133 E. Napa St., Sonoma, 95476 • Map L5 • 707 935 0576 • Open 11:30am–3pm & 5–9:30pm • $$$*

2 Harvest Moon Café
Their nightly menu features grilled pork sausages with pinquito beans, sautéed greens, and mustard sauce. ◊ *487 1st St. W., Sonoma, 95476 • Map L5 • 707 933 8160 • Open 5:30–9pm Wed–Mon (to 9:30pm Fri & Sat • $$$*

3 LaSalette
A modern take on traditional Portuguese cuisine is served here, with the focus very firmly on seafood. ◊ *452 1st St. E., Suite H, Sonoma, 95476 • Map L5 • 707 938 1927 • Open daily • $$$*

4 Petite Syrah
Seasonal Wine Country cuisine highlights the menu here. ◊ *205 5th St., Santa Rosa, 95401 • Map N2 • 707 568 4002 • Open 11:30am–2:30pm Mon–Sat, 5–10pm daily • $$$*

5 The Girl & the Fig
Savor their sweet breads with spring vegetables, sorrel vin blanc, or steamed mussels and fries. ◊ *110 W Spain St., Sonoma, 95476 • Map L5 • 707 938 3634 • Open 11:30am–10pm Mon–Thu, 10am–10pm Sun • $$$*

6 Basque Boulangerie Café
This charming little bistro serves sweet French breads, croissants, and seasonal pies and pastries, plus lunch. ◊ *460 1st St. E., Sonoma, 95476 • Map L5 • 707 935 7687 • Open 7am–6pm • $$*

7 Doce Lunas
The menu here includes crab cakes on spinach salad with ginger lime dressing, and braised lamb shank with herbs and garlic. ◊ *8910 Sonoma Hwy., Kenwood, 95452 • Map K4 • 707 833 4000 • Open 11:30am–8:30pm Wed–Sat, 10am–8:30pm Sun • $$$*

8 Juanita Juanita
Favored by local Hispanics, this restaurant offers all the Mexican favorites. ◊ *19114 Arnold Dr., Sonoma, 95476 • Map L5 • 707 935 3981 • Open 11am–8pm Wed–Mon • $$*

9 Café La Haye
Café La Haye delivers divine dishes fusing world influences to local ingredients. ◊ *140 E. Napa St., Sonoma, 95476 • Map L5 • 707 935 5994 • Open 5:30–9pm Tue–Sat • $$$*

10 Bistro 29
Warm and welcoming, Bistro 29 specializes in hearty Breton regional cuisine and local seafood. ◊ *620 5th St., Santa Rosa, 95404 • Map P1 • 707 546 2929 • Open 6am–6pm Mon–Thu, 6am–7pm Fri, 7am–7pm Sat, 7am–6pm Sun • $$$*

Left **Healdsburg Plaza** Center **Korbel Champagne Cellars** Right **HKG Estate Wines**

Russian River and Alexander Valley

THIS SPRAWLING REGION *is by far the most diverse area in Wine Country, with rolling meadows, redwood forests, and even beaches, as well as vales clad with vineyards and apple orchards. The hub is the handsome town of Healdsburg, in the upper Russian River Valley. To its southwest, the valley narrows as the river slices through the coastal mountains – a summer haven popular for fishing and canoeing, and for hiking in Armstrong Redwoods State Natural Reserve. East of Healdsburg, the sun-kissed Alexander Valley receives relatively few visitors, despite having vineyards whose grapes are renowned for producing wines with voluptuous flavors. The valley's boutique wineries include some of Wine Country's most prestigious names.*

Armstrong Redwoods Park

🔟 Sights

1. Ferrari-Carano Vineyards
2. Armstrong Redwoods State Natural Reserve
3. Gravenstein Highway
4. Guerneville
5. Healdsburg
6. Korbel Champagne Cellars
7. HKG Estate Wines
8. Francis Ford Coppola Winery
9. Russian River Jazz and Blues Festival
10. The River Road

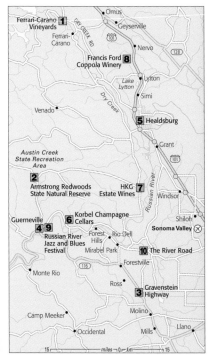

Preceding pages **Harvest season at Carneros vineyards, Napa**

Ferrari-Carano Vineyards

Set amid the rustic charm of the Dry Creek AVA and evoking the Tuscan landscape, Ferrari-Carano is notable for its pink Italianate mansion called *Villa Fiore* (House of Flowers). It is surrounded by manicured gardens where rows of tulips bloom in spring. A grand staircase leads down from the Mediterranean-style tasting room to the huge double-vaulted barrel cellars, where the winery's best wines can be tasted in the Enoteca Lounge. A complimentary wine-tasting pass can be downloaded from the website. ◈ *8761 Dry Creek Rd., Healdsburg, 95448 • Map H1 • 707 433 6700 • Open 10am–5pm • www. ferrari-carano.com*

Ferrari-Carano Vineyards

Armstrong Redwoods State Natural Reserve

This reserve protects 805 acres (330 ha) of Sequoia sempervirens – coast redwoods – including the 1,400 year-old Colonel Armstrong. The redwoods here tower 310 ft (95 m) skyward. Mystical fogs often shroud the forests, which thrive in the foggy coastal climate needed for the trees to survive. The level, 1.5-mile (2.5-km) long Pioneer Nature Trail leads to Colonel Armstrong and the Parson Jones Tree, the tallest in the grove (see pp26–7).

Gravenstein Highway

The "Gravenstein Highway" (SR-116) is named for the aromatic apple species grown around the towns of Sebastopol and Graton. Connecting Sebastopol to Forestville, it passes through a region of orchards producing Fuji, Golden Delicious, and Gravenstein apples. The latter grows particularly well in this area, although it is being replaced by other species. Many farms are open for visits. Pick up a free map from Sonoma County Farms. ◈ *www.farmtrails.com*

Guerneville

Surrounded by redwood and fir forests, Guerneville evolved as a 19th-century logging town: its annual town parade called "Stumptown Days" recalls the era. Guerneville is today the center of the "Russian Resort" area, drawing visitors for weekends of relaxation. It also has several gay resorts. Winters are cold and damp; summers are warm and dry, although fogs often seep in from the Pacific Ocean (see pp26–7).

The town of Guerneville

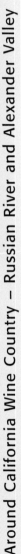

The Aroma Wheel

When tasting wine, being able to recognize its distinctive aromas adds to the enjoyment and appreciation. The Aroma Wheel makes the task easy. It categorizes aromas and bouquets (such as fruity) into sub-categories (such as citrus or berry) followed by specific examples (such as tangerine or blackberry). Many tasting rooms sell aroma wheels.

Healdsburg

Laid out in a grid around a Spanish-style plaza in the mid-1800s, Healdsburg's tree-shaded streets are lined with gracious Victorian homes, and many wine-tasting rooms surround the plaza. Many artists and musicians live here, adding to Healdsburg's cultural air, nightlife, and festivals. The Foss Creek Art Trail, still in development, displays outdoor artworks and art benches along a 4 mile (7 km) downtown walkway alongside the Northwestern Pacific Railroad and Foss Creek (see pp26–7).

Korbel Champagne Cellars

It is perhaps appropriate that this impressive winery is backed by redwood forest. It was founded in 1882 by three Czechoslovakian brothers, the

Korbel Champagne Cellars

Korbels, who had become wealthy in the redwood lumber industry. They concentrated on producing brandies and sparkling wines, as the modern winery still does. Winery tours are offered, and there is an interesting rose garden. Buy picnic supplies, along with wine or champagne, at the winery's delicatessen (see p26).

HKG Estate Wines

The Russian River was once a major hop-growing region and HKG Estate Wines has one of its best-preserved kilns. Built in 1905, the stone-and-timber structure, today serves as a wine-tasting room. This is one of the few local wineries producing wines from the once popular Napa Gamay grape. Visitors can also sample labels ranging from a delicate Gewürztraminer to an aptly-named Zinfandel-based "Big Red" (see pp26–7).

HKG Estate Wines

Francis Ford Coppola Winery

Sampling wines here takes a back seat to admiring the displays of iconic props from Hollywood producer – and winery owner – Francis Ford Coppola's famous movies. Look for Coppola's Oscars and other awards displayed atop the stairs above the reception *(see pp30–31)*.

Movie Memorabilia, Coppola Winery

Russian River Jazz and Blues Festival

Guerneville plays host to this world-renowned jazz concert, held at Johnson's Beach during the weekend after Labor Day. Bring camp chairs, swimwear, blankets, plus sunscreen and a hat, and enjoy listening to music performed by many of the world's finest jazz artistes, such as B.B. King and Chaka Khan *(see p27)*.
◈ www.russianriverfestivals.com

The River Road

South of Healdsburg, the Russian River turns west and carves a course through the coast range mountains. The Russian River Road parallels the river as it snakes through gorges and past wineries framed by stands of tall redwood trees. The road winds west through Guerneville and eventually emerges at the river mouth by the Pacific Ocean at Jenner. Bring a good map. ◈ *Map G3*

Drive Along the Russian River Road

Morning

Start out at Fulton, at the junction of the **River Road** and I-101, where the road begins. Heading west, you pass through a region of gently rolling meadows, orchards, and vineyards. Stop at Martinelli Winery to sample its Zinfandels and apple ciders. Reaching the "Long Snakes" (the local name for the river), stop at Steelhead Beach, a popular spot for canoeing and fishing. Don't miss **Korbel Champagne Cellars** *(see p26)* to sample its sparkling wines and to tour the rose garden. Its delicatessen sells gourmet sandwiches.

Afternoon

Passing through the quaint hamlet of Rio Nido, with its Tudor-style Rio Inn, arrive in **Guerneville** *(see p27)* with time to explore this laid-back town on foot. Be sure to walk the historic bridge, which leads from the main square and spans the river. Turn right in the center of town onto Armstrong Redwood Road to spend an hour or two sauntering the trails at **Armstrong Redwoods State Reserve** *(see p27)*. Suitably awed, drive through the park and ascend the steep switchback road to **Austin Creek State Recreation Area** *(see p92)*, which has more challenging hiking trails through oak woodland and along meandering streams. In late afternoon, return to the **River Road** and head west through the hamlets of Monte Vista – known for its Fourth of July fiesta – and Duncan Mills, which has Civil War reenactments, arriving at **Jenner** *(see p55)* and the Pacific Ocean in time for sunset.

Left **Healdsburg Museum** Right **The tiny hamlet of Geyserville**

TOP 10 Best of the Rest

1 Dry Creek Road
This road connects Healdsburg to Lake Sonoma. The narrow valley has many boutique wineries plus a few pear and prune orchards *(see p29)*.

2 Sebastopol
Known for its Gravenstein apples, this liberal community has peaceful streets graced with eclectic art. Luther Burbank's Gold Ridge Environmental Farm can be visited. ◎ *Map H4*

3 Austin Creek State Recreation Area
More than 20 miles (30 km) of trails meander the rolling hills and oak forests in this reserve. ◎ *17000 Armstrong Woods Rd., Guerneville, 95446 • Map G3 • 707 869 2015 • Adm*

4 Cloverdale Historical Museum
The Cloverdale Historical Society operates this small museum in the beautifully restored Gothic-Revival Gould Shaw House. Exhibits range from Pomo Indian baskets to antique farm implements. ◎ *215 N. Cloverdale Blvd., Cloverdale, 95425 • Map G1 • www.cloverdalehistory.org*

5 Jimtown Store
This country grocery store and deli is legendary for its wealth of wholesome goodies – from granola and spicy pepper jam to artisanal olive oils and gourmet wines. Boxed picnic lunches are available *(see p28)*.

6 Healdsburg Museum
Housed in the town library, this museum has exhibits that trace local history back to its Native American roots. ◎ *221 Matheson St., Healdsburg, 95448 • Map H2 • www.healdsburgmuseum.org*

7 Mud Bath at Osmosis Day Spa Sanctuary
Steep in a mixture of fine-ground and fermented cedar chips, rice bran, and plant enzymes, heated naturally by fermentation here. ◎ *209 Bohemian Hwy., Freestone, 95472 • Map H4 • www.osmosis.com*

8 Rio Nido Roadhouse
Relax with a glass of beer or wine and listen to locals blues, jazz, and rock bands in this bar and live music venue. ◎ *14540 Canyon Two Rd., 95471 • Map G3 • 707 869 0821 • Open 6pm–midnight Fri–Sun*

9 Johnson's Beach
This fun beach in the heart of Guerneville is hugely popular with families. A floating dam creates a still lagoon protected from the flow of the river. ◎ *16241 1st St., Guerneville, 95446 • Map G3 • www.johnsonsbeach.com*

10 Geyserville
At the north end of the Alexander Valley, this peaceful hamlet retains many of its mid-1800s structures. It has many noteworthy wineries and is a great base for exploring the valley by bicycle *(see p29)*.

Left **Stryker Sonoma vineyards** Right **Clos du Bois Winery**

TOP10 Wineries

1 Souverain
Occupying the Asti winery founded in the late 1800s, Souverain offers a tour that includes the original buildings, since retrofitted with modern wine production facilities *(see p29)*.

2 Clos du Bois Winery
The "Marlstone Experience" offers a tour through this winery's demonstration vineyard, plus a blending seminar. The tasting room is fashioned like a barn *(see p28)*.

3 Chalk Hill Estate
Opt for an educational estate tour that includes the vineyards, or a "Culinary Tour" featuring the winery's organic garden plus a sit-down food-and-wine pairing. ✆ *10300 Chalk Hill Rd., Healdsburg, 95448 • Map H2 • www.chalkhill.com*

4 Foppiano Vineyards
Having produced wines even through Prohibition, this small winery is still run by the founding family. Foppiano offers free tastings that include its distinctive high-tannic wines aged in American oak barrels *(see p27)*.

5 J Vineyards
Sparkling wines are J Vineyards' specialty. Their Bubble Room offers full-service tasting that includes six reserve wines paired with wine country fare. ✆ *11447 Old Redwood Hwy., Healdsburg, 95448 • Map H2 • www.jwine.com*

6 C.Donatiello Winery
Visit this boutique winery for its tiered herb gardens, and the relaxing tasting room – in a rustic redwood building overlooking the gardens and vineyards. ✆ *4035 Westside Rd., Healdsburg, 95448 • Map H2 • http://cdonatiello.com*

7 Thomas George Estates
Specializing in artisanal wines, this winery has its tasting room in a former hop kiln; a second tasting is held in the underground barrel cave. ✆ *8075 Westside Rd., Healdsburg, 95448 • Map H2 • 707 431 8031 • www. thomasgeorgeestates.com*

8 Iron Horse Vineyards
Approached by a palm- and olive-lined driveway, this rustic winery with a simple outdoor tasting room produces exceptional sparkling wines. ✆ *9786 Ross Station Rd., Sebastopol, 95472 • Map H4 • www.ironhorsevineyards.com*

9 Rodney Strong Vineyards
An educational tour of the vineyards and wine-making facility is offered here. Visitors can even try pruning vines or sugar testing grapes *(see p27)*.

10 Stryker Sonoma Winery
With a hospitality center noted for its glass and concrete contemporary architecture, this winery produces a vast portfolio of red wine varietals. ✆ *5110 Hwy. 128, Geyserville, 95441 • Map H1 • www.strykersonoma.com*

Left **Canoeing on the Russian River** Right **Armstrong Redwoods Reserve**

🔟 Outdoor Activities

1 Camping in Austin Creek State Recreation Area

This wilderness of meadows, oak woodlands, and tree-lined ravines is a perfect place to camp beneath the stars. ⊗ *Armstrong Woods Rd., 7 miles (11 km) N. of Guerneville • Map G3 • 707 869 2015 • Camping $25 per night per vehicle • www.parks.ca.gov*

2 Canoeing the Russian River

Rent a canoe or kayak for a 10-mile (16-km) self-guided paddle trip, with a shuttle pick-up at the end. ⊗ *Burke's Canoe Trips, 8600 River Rd., Forestville, 95436 • Map H3 • 707 887 1222 • www.burkescanoetrips.com*

3 Mountain Biking Lake Sonoma Recreation Area

Explore this wilderness recreation area by all-terrain bicycle along the 4-mile (7-km) Half-a-Canoe Loop Trail. ⊗ *3333 Skaggs Springs Rd., Geyserville, 95441 • Map H1 • 707 433 9483, 707 944 5500 • www.sonomauncorked.com*

4 Fishing

Try to catch Coho salmon and Steelhead trout in the Russian River. Lake Sonoma provides excellent fishing for bass and cat-fish anytime of the year. ⊗ *Map G1*

5 Hiking in Armstrong Redwoods Reserve

An easy Armstrong Nature Trail leads to the main redwood grove *(see p27)*. For more challenging hikes, take the East Ridge Trail, which ascends 1,500 ft (450 m) to Austin Creek State Recreation Area. ⊗ *Map G3*

6 Golfing

Redwood trees frame the fairways at the scenic nine-hole Northwood Golf Club. ⊗ *19400 Hwy. 116, Monte Rio, 95462 • Map G3 • 707 865 1116 • www.northwoodgolf.com*

7 Trail Rides

Explore the Russian River valley on horseback. Armstrong Woods Pack Station offers guided trail rides, plus 2- and 3-day pack trips. ⊗ *Box 287, Guerneville, 95446 • Map G3 • 707 887 2939 • www.redwoodhorses.com*

8 Segway Healdsburg

Take a Segway tour of the Russian River region, or a guided tour of the town, plus Dry Creek Valley and Armstrong Redwoods. ⊗ *790 Miramonte St., Healdsburg, 95448 • Map H2 • 707 953 3477 • www.segwayofhealdsburg.com*

9 Sonoma Canopy Tour

Strap into a harness and fly through the redwood treetops. The Sonoma Canopy Tour has seven ziplines. ⊗ *6250 Bohemian Hwy., Occidental, 95465 • Map H4 • 888 494 7868 • www.sonomacanopytours.com*

10 Hot-air Ballooning

Rising from the ground in a hot-air balloon then floating with the wind is an amazing adventure, and a unique way of exploring wine country *(see p48)*.

Price Categories

For a three course meal for one with half a bottle of wine (or equivalent meal), taxes and extra charges.

$	under $20
$$	$20–$40
$$$	$40–$55
$$$$	$55–$80
$$$$$	over $80

Left **A tasting session at Barndiva**

🔟 Places to Eat

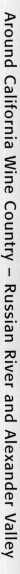

1 Redd
Feast on sashimi, pork belly, or duck breast paired with top Napa wines. ◈ 6480 Washington St., Yountville, 94599 • Map L4 • 707 944 2222 • Open 11:30am–2:30pm daily (from 11am Sun) & 5:30–9:30pm daily • $$$$$

2 Zin Restaurant & Wine Bar
The menu boasts seasonal American dishes from fresh local produce. ◈ 344 Center St., Healdsburg, 95488 • Map H2 • 707 473 0946 • Open 10am–11pm Sat, 11am–10pm Sun–Fri (to 11pm Fri, from 10am Sun) • $$$$

3 Boon Eat & Drink
Try the signature dish of deep-fried Brussels sprouts, and the Boon's Benedict breakfast. ◈ 16248 Main St., Guerneville, 95446 • Map G3 • 707 869 0780 • Open 11am–3pm & 5–9pm Thu–Sun (to 10pm Fri & Sat) • $$$

4 Ravenous Café & Lounge
Try the fish cakes with ginger-lemon-cilantro aioli. ◈ 420 Center St., Healdsburg, 95448 • Map H2 • 707 431 1302 • Open 11:30am–2:30pm & 5–9pm Wed–Sun • $$

5 Applewood Inn
Head here for comfort dishes, such as braised ham with parsley and roast potatoes. ◈ 13555 Hwy. 116, Guerneville, 95446 • Map G3 • 707 869 9093 • Dinner only • $$$

6 Willow Wood Market Café
This charming restaurant also has a bakery. Dine outside on sunny days. ◈ 9020 Graton Rd., Graton, 95444 • Map H3 • 707 823 0233 • Open 8am–9pm Mon–Sat, 9am–3pm Sun • $$

7 Himalayan Tandoori & Curry House
Authentic Indian and Nepalese/Himalayan food. ◈ 969 Gravenstein Hwy. S., Sebastopol, 95472 • Map H4 • 707 824 1800 • Open 11am–2pm & 5–9pm daily (Sun: dinner only) • $$

8 Bistro de Copains
This cozy restaurant offers seasonal dishes, such as steamed mussels in tomato, garlic, and pastis broth. ◈ 3782 Bohemian Hwy., Occidental, 95465 • Map H4 • 707 874 2436 • Open 5–9pm • $$$$

9 Scopa
Scopa's signature dish is the tomato-braised chicken. Local wines are served on Wednesday nights. ◈ 109 Plaza St. #A, Healdsburg, 95448 • Map H2 • 707 433 5282 • Open 5:30–10pm • $$$

10 Barndiva
Famous for its inventive cocktails, Barndiva also serves gourmet dishes. ◈ 231 Center St., Healdsburg, 95448 • Map H2 • 707 431 0100 • Open noon–9pm Wed–Sat, 11am–9pm Sun • $$$

Left **Camping at Hendy Woods State Park** Center **Weibel vineyards** Right **Hopland**

Mendocino and the Lake Counties

WINERIES EXTEND NORTHWEST *into the Anderson Valley of Mendocino County, stretching toward the Pacific Ocean, whose consistently cool, moist climate makes Mendocino Wine Country a realm of Gewürztraminer and other "green wine" grapes. Delightful B&B inns speckle the region, where deep valleys are shaded by majestic redwood forests, salmon swim in sparkling streams, and golden eagles soar overhead. The Anderson Valley is a gateway to the majestic Mendocino coastline. To the northeast, the vineyards of the upper Russian River Valley are interspersed with walnut and pear farms. The mountainous and thickly forested Lake Country region*

draws visitors to Clear Lake – the largest natural lake wholly within California. It offers fishing and other watersports.

Anderson Valley, Navarro Vineyards

TOP 10 Sights

1. Anderson Valley
2. Hopland
3. Weibel Family Vineyards
4. Parducci Wine Cellars
5. Ukiah
6. Navarro Vineyards
7. Mendocino Brewing Company
8. Boonville
9. Clear Lake
10. Hendy Woods State Park

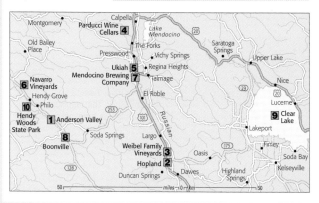

Anderson Valley

Drained by the Navarro River, this valley is a sparsely populated Shangri-La, with a delightful climate tempered by cool marine air that creeps in from the sea. SR-128 twists its way northwest between stands of redwood and fir trees, passing through scattered hamlets populated by aging hippies, old loggers, and a young breed of vintners with concern for the Earth. Its vineyards, which hug broad ridge-top plateaus and benches, produce world class Pinot Noir and Alsace varietals. ◈ Map A3

Hopland

This rustic farming community on the west bank of the Russian River is set amid oak covered hills. It is named for the hop-growing industry that flourished here for a century until it was killed off by mildew in the mid-1950s. The Hopland Band of Pomo Indians operates the Hopland Sho-Ka-Wah Casino on tribal lands east of town. Hopland is the main gateway to Clear Lake, via SR-175 which snakes uphill. ◈ Map C3 • www.shokawah.com

Weibel Family Vineyards

Founded in 1938 by Swiss immigrants, Weibel Family Vineyards is run by the fourth

Weibel Family Vineyards

generation of Weibels, who continue a family tradition of producing premium California sparkling wines from estate-grown Pinot Noir grapes, as well as a particular wine of note – Green Hungarian – first produced here in 1959 from a grape of obscure origin. The relaxed tasting room is welcoming, and visitors can marvel at the panoramic vineyard and valley views from a deck. ◈ 13275 South U.S. Hwy. 101, Hopland, 95449 • Map C3 • www.weibel.com

Parducci Wine Cellars

This boutique winery in the upper Russian River Valley is acclaimed for its earth-friendly practices, reflecting the owners' desire to create "America's Greenest Winery." Tours teach visitors about sustainable viticulture, such as how cover crops help attract beneficial insects and maintain soil vigor. The tasting room doubles as a delicatessen that sells picnic foods, which can be enjoyed on a garden patio with a fountain. Parducci also hosts special events. ◈ 501 Parducci Rd., Ukiah, 95482 • Map B1 • www.parducci.com

Parducci Winery

Redwoods

The California coast redwood is the tallest tree in the world, reaching up to 379 ft (115 m) in height. This rain-loving species of cypress can live to 2,000 years. It exists only in a narrow strip of land from southern Oregon to central California up to 50 miles (80 km) inland. It has thick, soft, fibrous rust-colored bark and the wood is naturally resistant to insects, fungi, and fire.

Navarro Vineyards

Ukiah

The former logging town of Ukiah is considered one of the most desirable places to live in California. Nestled in the Yokayo valley and protected from wind and fog by the Coast Mountain range, Ukiah is a center for pear orchards and for many of Mendocino County's best wineries. Lake Mendocino is nearby. ⊛ *Map C2*

Navarro Vineyards

Producers of some of the most acclaimed wines in Mendocino, Navarro Vineyards are known for their Gewürztraminers and Chardonnays. Founders Deborah Cahn and Ted Bennett chose their vineyard site in 1974

for its appropriate combination of climate and soils. Navarro specializes in aromatic varietals; tours include education on Navarro's babydoll sheep grazing, chicken tractor, and other sustainable agriculture projects. ⊛ *5601 Hwy. 128, Philo, 95466* • *Map A2* • *707 895 3686* • *www.navarrowine.com*

Mendocino Brewing Company

Established at Hopland in 1983 as California's first brewpub, the Mendocino Brewing Company was a pioneer in the USA's craft-beer renaissance. Now based in Ukiah, it produces flavor-rich beers named for local birds. Informative tours of the brewery are offered by appointment. Its Ale House is the perfect place to sample more than 20 different brews. ⊛ *1252 Airport Park Blvd., Ukiah, 95482* • *Map C2* • *707 467 2334* • *www.mendobrew.com*

Boonville

Founded in 1872, Boonville evolved as an agricultural center surrounded by orchards and ranches, many of which have been replaced by vineyards. The Anderson Valley Historical Museum, housed in an old one-room schoolhouse,

Mendocino Brewing Company

displays vintage farm equipment and memorabilia. The Anderson Valley Brewing Company offers tours of its microbrewery and sponsors the Boonville Beer Fest. ◎ *Map B3*

Clear Lake

California's largest freshwater lake formed 1.5 million years ago when tectonic movements sealed a valley that previously flowed into the Russian River. Measuring 19 miles (31 km) by 8 miles (13 km), the lake is considered the USA's foremost for bass-fishing. Clear Lake State Park, on the southwest shore, is popular for boating, fishing, water-skiing, and birding. ◎ *Map E3 • 707 279 4293*

Hendy Woods State Park

Hendy Woods State Park

Just 18 miles (28 km) northwest of Boonville, this majestic park protects two virgin groves of coast redwoods. These ancient groves are laced by self-guided trails. The Hermit Hut Trail leads to a crude hut made of redwood branches and once occupied by Hendy, a Russian-born hermit. The park has educational campfire programs, plus Junior Ranger nature walks for children. ◎ *18599 Philo-Greenwood Rd., Philo, 95466 • Map A2 • 707 895 3141 • Open 8am–sunset • www.parks.ca.gov*

One-day Drive along Hwy. 128

Morning

🕐 Start your drive in **Cloverdale** *(see p29)*, in the Alexander Valley, taking time to admire its Gothic Victorian homes before heading up Hwy. 128. The road soon begins to snake up and over the Yorkville Highlands to descend into the Navarro River valley. Approaching **Boonville**, turn right onto Boonville-Ukiah Rd. to visit the Anderson Valley Brewing Company, which has tours and a tasting room. Stop in **Boonville** to shop for picnic items at Farmhouse Mercantile. Also call at the Anderson Valley Historical Museum for a look at its eclectic exhibits tracing the history of the valley. Continue north on Hwy. 128 to Philo-Greenwood Rd. Turn left and follow the signs for **Hendy Woods State Park**, to hike the trails and enjoy a picnic lunch beneath the redwoods.

Afternoon

Call ahead to arrange a visit to Philo Apple Farm, at the junction of Philo-Greenwood Rd and Henry Woods State Park Rd. Returning to Hwy. 128, continue north for five minutes to **Navarro Vineyards**, on the right: a tour here is worthwhile. Another 2 miles (3 km) brings you to **Roederer Estate Winery** *(see p100)*: sample its premium sparkling wines. Further along, passing through the hamlet of Navarro, you enter an 11-mile (18-km) redwood tunnel alongside the Navarro River. It is a magnificent drive that leads to the mouth of the river and the Pacific Ocean.

Left **Roederer Estate Winery** Center **Paul Dolan wines** Right **Ukiah Brewing Company**

Husch Winery
This small, welcoming, family-operated winery's quaint tasting room is a converted 19th-century stable. ✆ *4400 Hwy. 128, Philo, 95466* • *Map A2* • *http://huschvineyards.com*

Kelseyville
Fondly called "Pearville," Kelseyville has flowering pear trees lining its Main St, with historic street lamps. It hosts a Pear Festival in September. ✆ *Lake County, 95451* • *Map E3*

Paul Dolan Vineyards
The winery owner is an expert on organic grape growing and wine making, and has authored two books on green practices in the wine industry. ✆ *501 Parducci Rd., Ukiah, 95482* • *Map B1* • *www.pauldolanwine.com*

Ukiah Brewing Company
Free live music nightly, the brewery's seven made-on-site beers, and great pub food using all-organic ingredients, are all good reasons to visit here. ✆ *102 S. State St., Ukiah, 95482* • *Map C2* • *www.ukiahbrewingco.com*

Highway 128
Snaking a route through the Anderson and Navarro River Valleys, this scenic highway leads to pristine redwood forests and, eventually, the Mendocino coast. Most sites of interest in the two valleys lie along this route. ✆ *Map A2*

Greenwood Ridge Vineyards
Award-winning, estate-bottled wines can be sampled in the octagonal tasting room made from the lumber of a single redwood tree. ✆ *5501 Hwy. 128, Philo, 95466* • *Map A2* • *www.greenwoodridge.com*

Roederer Estate Winery
Antiques adorn the stone-and-timber tasting room here, with a gallery of celebrity photos. ✆ *4501 Hwy. 128, Philo, 95466* • *Map A2* • *www.roedererestate.com*

Montgomery Woods State Reserve
This reserve protects the massive Sierra Redwood (Sequoia giganteum), and the taller coast redwood (Sequoia sempervirens). ✆ *Orr Springs Rd., 13 miles (21 km) W. of Ukiah, 95482* • *Map A1* • *707 937 5804* • *Open 8am–sunset*

Mailliard Redwoods State Reserve
The drive through the old-growth redwood groves in this small mountainside park in the Garcia River Valley is inspirational. ✆ *Hwy. 122, 3 miles (5 km) W. of Hwy. 128, Yorkville, 95494* • *Map B4* • *707 937 5804*

Germain-Robin Distillery
Tastings are by appointment in this distillery, which produces brandies and grappa using an antique still and fine grapes. ✆ *3001 S. State St. Ukiah, 95482* • *Map C2* • *www.germain-robin.com*

Price Categories

For a three-course meal for one with half a bottle of wine (or equivalent meal), taxes and extra charges.	
$	under $20
$$	$20–$40
$$$	$40–$55
$$$$	$55–$80
$$$$$	over $80

Left **The Himalayan Café**

Places to Eat

Bluebird Café
This small café is known for its exotic meat burgers and delicious fruit pies. ◈ *13340 S. Hwy. 101, Hopland, 95449 • Map C3 • 707 744 1633 • Open 7am–2pm Mon–Thur, 7am–7pm Fri–Sun • $$*

Laurens Café
Burgers, pizzas, pastas, and sandwiches are made here using garden-fresh ingredients. ◈ *14211 Hwy. 128, Boonville, 95415 • Map B3 • 707 895 3869 • Open 5–9pm Tue–Sat, 11:30am–2:30pm Thur–Sun • $$$*

Libby's
A Mexican restaurant with all the usual staples, such as burritos and carnitas, plus seafood specials. ◈ *8651 Hwy. 128, Philo, 95466 • Map A2 • 707 895 2646 • Open noon–2pm & 6–9pm Tue–Sat • $$*

Boont Berry Farm
Pastries, salads, sandwiches, and vegan dishes are on offer here. ◈ *13981 Hwy. 128, Boonville, 95415 • Map B3 • 707 895 3576 • Open 10am–6pm Mon–Fri • $$*

Table 128
Their prix fixe menu includes pan-seared flat-iron steak with basque chili cream and creamy polenta. ◈ *14050 Hwy. 128, Boonville, 95466 • Map B3 • 707 895 2210 • Call ahead for times • $$$*

The Philo Apple Farm
Set amid its own apple orchards, this farm also sells cider and chutneys and doubles as a cooking school. ◈ *18501 Greenwood Rd., Philo, 95466 • Map A2 • 707 895 2333 • Call ahead for times*

Oco Time
This local favorite serves sushi, noodles, *tempura*, and dinner platters. ◈ *111 W. Church St., Ukiah, 95482 • Map C3 • 707 462 2411 • Open 11:30am–2:15pm Tue–Fri, 5:30–8:30pm Mon–Sat (to 9pm Fri & Sat) • $$$*

Patrona Restaurant
The menu here focuses on hyper-local dishes that pair Mendocino ingredients with local wines. ◈ *130 West Standley St., Ukiah, 95482 • Map C2 • 707 462 9181 • Open 11am–9:30pm Tue–Sat • $$$*

Oco Time
Run by a Japanese-born couple, this restaurant's full Japanese menu includes sushi. ◈ *111 West Church St., Ukiah, 95482 • Map C2 • 707 462 2422 • Call ahead for times • $$$$*

The Himalayan Café
Try the chef's special: fire-roasted eggplant in spices and cream. ◈ *1639 South State St., Ukiah, 95482 • Map C2 • 707 467 9900 • Open noon–2pm Tue–Fri, 5–8:30pm Mon–Sat • $$*

Around California Wine Country – Mendocino and the Lake Counties

Discover more at **www.dk.com**

STREETSMART

CALIFORNIA WINE COUNTRY'S TOP 10

Left **Wine tasting, Castello di Amorosa** Center **Napa Valley** Right **Charles M. Schulz Museum**

ⁱ⁰ Planning Your Trip

When to Go
Wine Country is busiest in summer months. In spring, the mustard fields are ablaze with yellow blossoms. Fall is the best time for winery tours, when the wineries are busy with the harvest. Winter months are less crowded, and prices are lower.

Passports and Visas
Visitors from abroad must have a valid passport to enter the USA. Many nationalities also require a non-immigrant visa. Australian, British, and Canadian citizens plus people from other Visa Waiver Program countries do not need visas for stays of up to 90 days.
⊗ US State Department
• www.travel.state.gov/visa

Insurance
It is wise to get insurance for loss or theft of valuables as well as for trip cancellation and full medical coverage, including repatriation by air. Visitors intending to participate in adventure sports should be sure that their policy covers these activities.

Climate
Wine Country has several microclimates, and conditions can vary greatly within a short distance. Temperatures rise with distance from the coast and San Francisco Bay: Calistoga,

for example, is several degrees warmer than Napa. The fog-bound Anderson and Navarro Valleys of Mendocino, and the lower Russian River Valley are cooled by moist ocean air. Most rain falls between November and April.

What to Pack
If you're visiting during the summer months, take light clothing to beat the midday heat. A sweater is needed for evenings, even in summer, and a warm rainproof jacket is a must in winter. Dressy clothes are required in fancy restaurants. Do not forget sunscreen and a shade hat.

Choosing an Area
Napa Valley attracts the bulk of visitors and has the most variety, from mud-bath spas to ballooning and bicycling. Sonoma Valley and Santa Rosa are rich in museums and cultural draws. Choose the Russian River and Mendocino regions for rugged adventures, with their redwood forest and boutique wineries.

How Long to Stay
It is best to combine two or three areas of the Wine Country to gain a full sense of the region, and to appreciate the distinctions of its wines. Allow at least two days for Napa Valley and one day for Sonoma Valley. The far northern regions,

such as Mendocino, span greater distances than the Napa and Sonoma Valleys, so allow adequate time.

Disabled Travelers
By law, hotels, restaurants, and public buildings must provide wheelchair access, and many have special bathroom facilities. Public buses are also equipped to handle wheelchairs, and sidewalks in most towns have wheelchair ramps. ATMs have braille touch buttons.

Traveling with Children
Children are not welcome at wineries, and anyone under 21 may not consume alcohol. Still, Wine Country has plenty of family-friendly places, such as Safari West (see p25), the Charles M. Schulz Museum (see p24), and the Francis Ford Coppola Winery (see pp30–31). Some hotels may charge an extra bed rate for children under 16.

Further Reading
Read Jack London's *The Valley of the Moon* and R.L. Stevenson's *The Silverado Squatters* to gain a greater appreciation for Wine Country. Eyewitness Companions *Wines of the World* and *Wine Country Cooking* by Joanne Wier will help you appreciate the region's wines and cuisines.

Left **San Francisco airport shuttle** Right **Limousine tour**

🔟 Arriving in Wine Country

Domestic Flights
American Airlines, United, and Virgin America are among the airlines offering regular flights to San Francisco from around the US. Alaska Airlines, Delta Air Lines and Southwest Airlines have flights to Oakland. Alaska Airlines also flies direct to Charles M. Schulz Sonoma County Airport, in Santa Rosa, from Las Vegas, Los Angeles, Portland, and Seattle. 🌐 www.aa.com; www.united.com; www.virginamerica.com; www.alaskaair.com; www.delta.com; www.southwest.com

Domestic Airports
San Francisco airport and Oakland airport are served by domestic flights from around the US. Additionally, consider flying into Sacramento airport (SMF), about 60 miles (97 km) east of Napa. Small aircraft can also be chartered for flights into regional airstrips, such as Napa, Healdsburg, and Ukiah.

Airport Shuttle Links
Evans Transportation has nine daily shuttles between Napa and San Francisco airport, and six shuttles daily to/from Oakland airport, using modern air-conditioned coaches. No reservations are required. 🌐 707 255 1559 • Cash only • www.evanstransportation.com

International Flights
More than two dozen major airlines offer direct flights from Europe to San Francisco and Los Angeles. British Airways, Virgin Atlantic, and many other airlines also fly to various US cities, where you can take a connecting flight to San Francisco or Oakland. The flight time between London and San Francisco is 10 hours. 🌐 www.britishairways.com; www.virgin-atlantic.com

International Airports
San Francisco International Airport (SFO) and Oakland airport (OAK) are the closest international airports to Wine Country. Both are about a one-hour drive from Napa and Sonoma.

Duty-Free Allowances
Visitors to the USA may bring 200 cigarettes or 50 cigars (of non-Cuban origin) plus one liter of alcoholic beverages. For information on prohibited items, check the US Customs & Border Patrol website. 🌐 www.cbp.gov/xp/cgov/travel/id_visa

Long-Distance Buses
Greyhound operates a long-distance bus service to San Francisco from across the US, with a connector service to Santa Rosa. Marin Airporter operates a scheduled bus service between San Francisco International Airport and six Marin County destinations every 30 minutes (5am–midnight). 🌐 www.greyhound.com; www.marinairporter.com

By Rail
Amtrak offers intercity train services to Sacramento, Oakland, and San Francisco from across the US, with a connecting bus service to Napa, Santa Rosa, Petaluma, Healdsburg, and Cloverdale. 🌐 www.amtrak.com

By Car
High-speed freeways connect California to all the neighboring states. The Interstate 101 (I-101) freeway links San Francisco to Oregon via Santa Rosa, Healdsburg, and the Upper Russian River Valley. SR-29 connects Napa and the Napa Valley to Interstate 80 (I-80), which links Oakland to Sacramento and Nevada. All international airports have car rental agencies.

By Limousine
Several limousine companies specialize in chauffeured tours of wine country. Service is usually door to door. 🌐 Classic Limousine, 572 Lincoln Av, Napa, 94558 • 707 253 0999 • www.classiclimousine.50megs.com

After arriving on an international flight, allow time to relax before hiring a rental car.

Left **Napa Valley bike tour** Right **Baylink Ferry**

Getting Around

By Car/RV
It is easiest to get around Wine Country by car, particularly in the more remote Mendocino and Lake County regions. Most sites of interest lie along major routes, but others are tucked away on narrow and sometimes confusing country lanes, so bring a good map. In small and medium-size towns, it is best to park the car and explore on foot.

Renting a Car
Reserve a car ahead of your arrival. Most major car rental companies have offices in the international airports, with regional outlets in Santa Rosa and Napa. Also, consider renting an RV (recreational vehicle) – a campervan fully equipped with kitchen and beds – capable of sleeping 4–8 people. RVs give you the freedom to camp in wilderness areas.

Road Rules
Be aware of local road rules that may not be familiar to you in your home country. It is illegal to pass a car on the right side. Passing on the left is only allowed when there is a broken line in the middle of the road and there is clear visibility. The California Department of Motor Vehicles publishes the California Driver Handbook. ⚲ dmv. ca.gov/pubs/hdbk

Gasoline
Self-service gas (petrol) stations are located in all towns and along major highways. Don't let your tank get close to empty when driving in Mendocino and Lake Counties, where stations are sporadic. Arco stations typically have the lowest prices.

Buses
Golden Gate Transit operates a comprehensive bus service throughout Marin County and southern Sonoma County. The Napa County Transportation & Planning Agency (NCTPA) has seven interlinked shuttle routes throughout Napa Valley, and a commuter bus links Napa to the Vallejo ferry terminal and BART rail network. ⚲ www.goldengate.org; www.nctpa.net

Organized Tours
There are plenty of tours on offer – by bus, limousine, bicycle, and on foot (see p112). California Wine Tours specializes in scheduled and customized tours of Napa and Sonoma Valleys. ⚲ www. californiawinetours.com

By Bicycle
Bicycling offers a healthy and enjoyable way of exploring Wine Country at a relaxed pace. The Silverado Trail is an ideal route through Napa Valley. You can rent bicycles from Sonoma Valley Cyclery, and from Napa Valley Bike Tours, which has guided tours. ⚲ www.napavalleywine tours.com; www.sonoma cyclery.com

By Taxi
Taxis are available in larger towns and work on a metered basis. Taxi drivers are also open to setting a fee for long sightseeing journeys by the hour or day. However, touring by taxi can be expensive and may only be sensible if shared by several people.

By Boat
Baylink Ferries operates 12 high-speed ferries daily on weekdays, and seven daily on weekends, between San Francisco and Vallejo, from where you can take a bus to Napa. You can also take a Golden Gate Ferry from San Francisco to Sausalito or Larkspur, and catch a public bus or hire a taxi to Sonoma or Santa Rosa. ⚲ www. baylinkferry.com; www. goldengate.org

Walking
Do not miss the opportunity to explore the various sights of the region on foot. Wear comfortable shoes. California law permits pedestrians to cross city streets only at specified crossings, and police issue fines for "jay-walking." Most parks have trails for hiking.

Left **Bookstore** Center **Signage, California Welcome Center** Right **Visitors Bureau, Sonoma**

Sources of Information

Tourist Offices

The California Travel and Tourism Commission issues a visitors' guide and has Welcome Centers throughout the state, including in Santa Rosa. The different regions of Wine Country also have tourism offices, where you can pick up literature and get advice.

- www.visitcalifornia.com
- www.visitcwc.com
- www.napavalley.com
- www.sonomavalley.com
- www.russianriver.com
- www.visitmendocino.com

Winery Associations

The wineries of the region are represented by several separate organizations. Some also mail out literature, and a few have tourist information bureaus. Napa Valley Vintners and Sonoma County Wineries Association are among the most important.

- www.napavintners.com
- www.sonomawine.com
- www.wineroad.com
- www.mendowine.com

Hotel Associations

The California Hotel and Lodgings Association and California Association of Bed and Breakfast Inns can provide information about member hotels throughout the state. The Bed and Breakfast Inns of Napa Valley and the Bed and Breakfast Association of Sonoma Valley provide information about their member hotels.

- www.calodging.com
- www.cabbi.com
- www.bbinv.com
- www.sonomabb.com

Local Tour Operators

Found throughout the region, local tour operators are often the most reliable sources of information about sightseeing and activities related to specific areas and destinations. Many companies also operate tourist information bureaus.

Bookstores and Libraries

Several bookstores in Wine Country have a good range of guidebooks, maps, and other travel-related literature. Hotel gift stores are also good sources, as are local libraries. The Sonoma County Wine Library (see p47) is the best resource for books about wine and viticulture.

Websites

There is a huge amount of information about Wine Country available online. Google and other Internet search engines are a useful means of locating specific information, such as weather conditions, the cost of flights, etc.
- www.winecountry.com

Maps

There are several good maps of California Wine Country. The free maps offered at tourist offices and most hotels are all that most people need. Detailed maps of wineries can be downloaded from the internet.
- www.winecountry.com/maps

Local Publications

Several local newspapers publish articles and news about Wine Country, such as the *Napa Valley Register*, the *St. Helena Star*, and *Santa Rosa Press Democrat*, available at newsstands. Regional magazines include *Napa Sonoma Magazine* and *Savor Wine Country*. Most are available online and some are available free in hotels.

Guides

There are many well-informed and qualified guides available. Ask local travel agencies or your hotel concierge to recommend a reliable guide. Many taxi drivers also hire themselves out as guides.

Weather Reports

Real-time weather reports are available online, some of which provide weather forecasts for up to one week ahead. Local newspapers and TV news channels also provide short- and long-term weather forecasts.
- www.weather.com
- http://forecast.weather.gov

Left **Pet carrier** Center **No smoking sign** Right **A 20-dollar banknote**

10 Practical Information

Time Zones
California is three hours behind US Eastern Standard Time (EST) and eight hours behind Greenwich Mean Time (GMT). Daylight Saving Time is observed between the second Sunday in March and the first Sunday in November.

Opening Hours
Most shops in big cities open at 9, 10, or 11am and close at 6pm, with later closing on Fridays and Saturdays and reduced hours on Sundays. Banks also have variable hours but are usually open 9am–5pm weekdays and 9am–1pm Saturday. Call ahead for opening times at specific locations.

Admission Charges
Many art galleries, museums, and state parks permit free entry, including wineries that have art collections or specialist museums. Other museums charge between $5 and $10, and some state parks charge $8 per vehicle entry. Most wineries charge a $5–25 tasting fee; some offer free tasting.

Public Holidays
Most businesses close for public holidays. Nearly all wineries are open daily, as are tourist information bureaus and many restaurants, except for Thanksgiving and Christmas and New Years Day, when public transportation operates a restricted service. If you plan on dining out, reserve well in advance.

Taxes and Tipping
A service charge may be included in your bill at many restaurants. If it is not, a 15–20 percent tip is customary. There are no set rates for hotel staff, but $1 per bag is considered correct for porters and $1 per day for maids. Taxi drivers are usually tipped 10 percent. All purchases have a sales tax, which ranges from 8.5 to over 10 percent.

Smoking
Smoking is banned in all public buildings, including offices, restaurants, and bars. Many restaurants have outside patios reserved for smokers. No minor can purchase tobacco products, which are sold in groceries and supermarkets throughout Wine Country.

Electrical Appliances
The electricity supply works mostly on a 110-volt system. A few outlets are 220 volts – these are usually marked. Plugs have two flat pins, so visitors from Europe will need adaptors. Power outages are rare, but a surge protector is a good investment for laptop computers.

Traveling with Pets
Most hotels and restaurants ban dogs and other pets, although exceptions are made for guide dogs. You can check online for hotels that welcome dogs. Most domestic airlines will permit you to travel with a dog or cat; contact your airline for full details. ⊗ www.dogfriendly.com; www.bringfido.com

Photography
Most museums allow photography, but flash is usually banned and tripods barred in several places. In Santa Rosa, Shutterbug Cameras and Jeremiah's Photo Corner stock photographic equipment, but dedicated camera shops are otherwise few and far between in Wine Country. ⊗ Shutterbug Cameras: 3011 Santa Rosa Av., 95407; Map J3; 707 546 3456; Open 9am–6pm Mon–Fri, 9am–5pm Sat, 10am–5pm Sun; www.shutterbugcamerashops.com • Jeremiah's Photo Corner: 441 Sebastopol Av., 95401; Map J3; 707 544 4800; Open 10am–6pm Tue–Fri, 10am–5pm Sat; www.jeremiahsphotocorner.com

Money
Almost all retail outlets accept payment by credit or debit card, but it is wise to always carry sufficient US dollar currency for small purchases, and fares for buses and taxis.

Left **ATM** Center **San Francisco Chronicle** Right **Mailbox**

Top 10 Banking and Communications

1 The US Dollar
The US dollar is the local currency. It is divided into 100 cents, with coins in denominations of 1, 5, 10, 25, and 50 cents, and notes of 1, 2, 5, 10, 20, 50, and 100 dollars in circulation.

2 Foreign Currency
You can bring an unlimited amount of foreign currency into the USA. Some entities, such as factory outlets, may accept payment in Euros or Sterling, but these are the exception. Major foreign currencies can be exchanged at banks and hotel reception desks.

3 Banks and ATMs
Every town has several US banks with ATMs, such as Bank of America and Wells Fargo, and many small communities have at least one local bank. Most change foreign currencies at the official exchange rate.

4 Credit Cards
MasterCard and VISA are accepted in virtually all hotels, restaurants, and tourist-oriented stores and businesses, but not all places accept American Express or Discover. A few smaller restaurants, however, accept cash only. Credit cards can be used for cash advances at banks, though you may be charged a commission. You can also use them at ATMs, so memorize your personal identification number (PIN) before leaving for your trip.

5 Telephones
Public phones are quite rare these days. It is possible to buy a disposable cell phone with prepaid minutes from a supermarket or convenience store. Calls from hotels can be expensive. To call North America from the UK, dial 00 for international access, followed by 01, then the local number. All phone numbers in the USA have a 3-digit area code, which varies by region throughout Wine Country.

6 Cellphones
AT&T, Sprint, T-Mobile, and Verizon offer cellular service throughout the Wine Country region. However, do not count on your cell phone working in some of the relatively remote locations. All these companies have offices and phone centers in major cities.

7 Post Offices
The US Postal Service offers speedy and efficient service. Every town has a post office. Check with the reception staff of your hotel to see if they can forward your mail to the post office. Most post offices open 9am–5pm Monday to Friday; some open 9am–noon Saturday.

8 Internet and WiFi
Most hotels provide WiFi or modem connections in guest rooms, although some charge a fee. Others limit their Internet service to public lounges. Many cafés and some restaurants also have free WiFi service, as do libraries. Internet cafés are widely available and charge reasonable rates.

9 Newspapers
The *San Francisco Chronicle* is the major regional daily newspaper, but *USA Today* and other national newspapers are sold at newsagents and newsstands. The local *Napa Valley Register* and Santa Rosa *Press Democrat* are also dailies, and the *St. Helena Star* is published weekly; all have a strong regional focus and are available online.

10 TV and Radio
Most hotels include cable TV in room rates, with international channels such as CNN. Premium channels such as HBO may be available on a pay-per-view basis. Dozens of radio stations span the spectrum from country music to rock and easy listening, although many have limited range, and in more remote parts of Mendocino and Lake County relatively few stations may be available.

Left **Hospital, Napa** Center **Police car** Right **Pharmacy delivery car**

🔟 Security and Health

1 Emergencies
In an emergency, dial 911 for fire, police, or medical assistance. Hotels can also arrange for a doctor or ambulance.

2 Health Services
Local health standards are of a high quality. There are hospitals in most cities, and doctors and clinics in smaller towns. Your hotel should be able to recommend a doctor. Invest in insurance, as fees for medical services in the U.S. are extremely high. Most health-insurance plans are accepted, but those who do not have coverage may be denied service.

3 Dental Care
California has a very efficient dental infra-structure, and most towns have a choice of private dentists. Ensure that your travel insurance covers dental care, as it is expensive. 🌐 *www.californiadentists.com*

4 Pharmacies
It is always a good idea to bring along enough prescription medicines to last the duration of your stay. Still, there are plenty of pharmacies throughout California. Check with U.S. Customs in advance to ensure that any prescription medicines you wish to bring from overseas are allowed.

5 Police
California Highway Patrol (CHP) vehicles patrol major highways, and local police patrol cities. The police are highly efficient and professional and most cities have their own police force, in addition to County Sheriff's departments.
🌐 *Napa: 707 257 9550*
• *Sonoma: 707 996 3602*
• *Santa Rosa: 707 543 4550*
• *Healdsburg: 707 431 3377*

6 Drinking and Driving
The CHP and local police strictly enforce drink-driving laws, and sobriety checkpoints are frequently set up. Avoid drinking and driving. If you plan on wine-tasting, temper your intake, drink plenty of water, and consider designating a non-drinking driver. Call 911 if you spot a drunk driver.

7 Outdoors Concerns
Protect yourself against California's intense summer sun: use sunscreens and carry a shade hat when spending time outdoors. Back-country hikers should be on the lookout for rattlesnakes and poison-oak *(see p111)*, and be aware that mountain lions are found in many wilderness areas. Stay on marked trails. There are few biting insects in Wine Country.

8 Earthquakes
Although extremely rare, the possibility of a severe earthquake is an ever-present danger in Wine Country, which lies close to the San Andreas Fault. If a major earthquake occurs, take cover under something sturdy if you are indoors, keep away from glass and walls, and do not use elevators. If you're outdoors, stay away from buildings and tall objects. If driving, stop your vehicle in an open space away from utility wires.

9 Wildfires
In summer months, the high temperatures and lack of rain can cause fast-moving forest wildfires, often fanned by hot winds. On such occasions, roads may be closed and mandatory evacuation orders may be enforced. Never hike in areas close to wildfires. Extinguish cigarettes properly and adhere to local regulations regarding campfires.

10 Women Travelers
Women are treated fully as equals in California and undue flirting is not present. Still, common sense precautions are wise for women travelers. Avoid walking alone at night, especially in dark places or places where help may not be available, and leave expensive jewelry at home.

➡ *Black widow spiders and brown recluse spiders are present in Wine Country and can give bites that produce severe reactions.*

Left **Rattlesnake** Right **Traffic jam on Highway 29, Napa Valley**

TOP 10 Things to Avoid

1 Drugs
Marijuana is a major, but illegal, cash crop and although smoking it may be tolerated by a large part of the community, the police take a different view. Buying and dealing drugs is dangerous – getting caught will ruin your vacation.

2 Over-Indulgence
Sampling wines at several wineries is enjoyable, but the effects can creep up on you. Although servings are small, each sample adds up. Limit yourself to tasting at select wineries, stretch out your tastings over several hours, and drink plenty of water.

3 Traffic Jams
Most people who choose to explore Napa Valley do so along Hwy 29, which can be thronged with vehicles on weekends and public holidays, especially in summer. On those days, take the Silverado Trail (see pp18–19) or consider exploring less-visited areas, such as the Alexander Valley.

4 Poison Oak
"Poison oak" grows throughout wine country and is prevalent in oak, fir, and redwood forests. This bush can cause irritating rashes as well as serious allergic reactions upon contact with human skin. The vine's leaves have three pointed leaflets with a longer central stem but can take many forms. They are red in spring, green in summer, and vary from yellow to maroon in fall.

5 Pickpockets
Crime against visitors is relatively rare in Wine Country. However, precautions must be taken when in crowded places and city centers. Carry a handbag with a cross-body strap and keep it zipped, put your wallet in the zippered pocket, and always stay aware of your surroundings.

6 Rattlesnakes
Northern Pacific rattlesnakes are often encountered along hiking and bike trails, and in grassland and even urban settings. Their venom is potentially fatal, and anyone who is bitten should seek immediate medical assistance. Do not put your hands under rocks or other objects where snakes like to hide, and keep a safe distance from snakes you may encounter on trails.

7 Dressing Inappropriately
Although shorts are normally permitted, most wineries have a dress code, which may include a ban on tank tops for men. Check with particular wineries about their policies, especially for wine-pairing dinners. Avoid wearing perfume or cologne, which can interfere with the tasting experience. Most upscale restaurants require long pants for men.

8 Lost Property
If you lose an item of value, check with the places you last visited, as it may be held in safe-keeping. If not, report it to the local police in the hope that someone finds it and returns it; in which case, the police can contact you.

9 Dehydration
Summers in Wine Country can be hot, and it is important to stay hydrated by drinking sufficient water. This is especially true if you are drinking alcohol and if you participate in any strenuous activities, such as hiking or biking. At least 3 liters (8 pints) of water a day is recommended in summer.

10 Peak Times
Many local San Francisco Bay Area residents head to Wine Country on weekends, especially in summer and during public holidays. It is best to avoid these times, when you should plan on visiting more remote regions. Make your reservations early for this period. Winter and early spring are good times to visit and are generally uncrowded.

 Wear comfortable flat-soled shoes for wine-tasting, as you may be standing at a bar for long periods of time.

Left **Napa Valley Wine Train tour** Center **Culinary Institute of America** Right **Hiking trail**

Tours and Special Interests

Winery Tours
Almost every winery welcomes visitors and most charge a fee for wine-tasting, which can vary from $5 to $25. Off-the-beaten-track wineries may offer complimentary tasting. Many offer optional tours for an extra fee, or include tasting as part of obligatory tours that may include visits to historic caves, and which provide an educational background that permits you to better appreciate the wines being tasted.

Food Tours
The Culinary Institute of America (see pp16–17) offers tours of its world-renowned academy, while Food and Wine Trails offers a three-day epicurean tour of the valley, including the Napa Valley Wine Train (see pp12–13), which combines a tour of the valley with a fine-dining experience. ◉ www.foodandwinetrails.com

Bicycle Tours
Napa Valley Bike Tours offers four guided itineraries in Napa Valley and also plans customized self-guided itineraries. Backroads has trips in the Alexander Valley and an all-Wine Country trip. A support wagon carries your luggage on group trips. ◉ www.backroads.com

River Tours
Dolphin Charters offers boat excursions on the Napa and Petaluma Rivers, providing a relaxing and romantic way to explore southern sections of Wine Country. You can paddle along the Napa River with Kayak Napa Valley, which offers guided kayak trips. ◉ www.dolphincharters.com; www.kayaknv.com

Limousine Tours
Limousine tours are a popular way to explore the Napa and Sonoma Valleys and offer the benefit of not having to worry about drinking and driving. Most companies, such as Appellation Tours, offer a choice of vehicles, from stretch limos to large SUVs. ◉ Appellation Tours: 510 527 9622; www.appellationtours.com

Cooking Schools
The Inn at Ramekin's (see p60) has four-day culinary camps and offers private classes focusing on local ingredients and "Wine Country Cuisine." The Culinary Institute of America (see pp16–17) offers cooking classes, one- to five-day courses, plus long-term, degree-level programs.

Gourmet Dining
Many notable chefs have established world-class restaurants in the Wine Country region. Book well ahead, as the best restaurants are extremely popular, and patrons are known to drive two hours or more for the experience. The top-tier restaurants, such as the French Laundry (see p75), require reservations months in advance.

Birding
With many distinct ecosystems, Wine Country is a mecca for birders. Opportunities vary by season, as many birds are temporary migrants. Bald eagles are often spotted in winter. The Napa-Solano Audubon Society has birding field trips. ◉ www.napasolano audobon.com

Hiking
Wine Country's many natural parks and preserves offer bountiful opportunities for hiking, from the easy walks of Armstrong Redwoods State Natural Reserve (see p27) to the demanding hike to the summit of Mount St. Helena (see p51). Wear sturdy but lightweight hiking shoes, and take water. You can join hikes offered by the Sierra Club.

Ballooning
Wine Country Balloons and Balloons Over the Valley are among the several companies that offer tours by hot-air balloon, which typically lift-off around dawn, ascend as high as 3,300 ft (1,000 m), and end with a champagne toast. All pilots are licensed. ◉ www.balloontours.com; www.balloonrides.com

Left **Oxbow Public Market** Right **Camping at Hendy Woods State Park**

🔟 Dining and Accommodation Tips

1 Types of Restaurants
Cafés range from single coffee-shops to full-service restaurants that are often the best option around for breakfasts. Many Wine Country restaurants are French-style bistros – relaxed eateries serving regional Wine Country dishes.

2 Produce Markets
Almost every town in Wine Country has a farmers' market at least one day a week most months. Grocery stores stock fresh-picked fruit and vegetables. Oakville Grocery (see p73) and Oxbow Public Market (see p73) are two of the best. Many wineries have well-stocked delicatessens.

3 Health Food Stores
Organic products are easy to find in Wine Country. Nature Select Foods, in St. Helena, sells all manner of herbs and health food products. Whole Foods supermarket chain specializes in organic produce and has stores in Napa, Petaluma, Sonoma, and Santa Rosa.

4 Vegetarians
Most restaurants in Wine Country feature vegetarian dishes on their menus. Some restaurants specialize in serving vegetarians and vegans – people who eat no animal-derived products, such as cheeses. Try Pica Pica, an upscale food stand in Napa's Oxbow Market, serving gluten-free, vegan, and non-vegan South-American cuisine.
🌐 www.picapica.com

5 Brewpubs
Microbreweries – small breweries that specialize in artisanal beers – abound in Northern California. Many are associated with brewpubs that brew their own beer and serve beer-friendly food. Live music is a staple. Some brewpubs offer beer tasting; the Silverado Brewing Company even has a five-course brewer's dinner with beer pairings.

6 Types of Accommodation
Accommodations range from charming B&Bs and cozy country inns furnished with antiques to sophisticated spa resorts and contemporary styled boutique hotels. You can also opt for cottage and villa rentals. Lodgings are as varied in price as they are in style.

7 B&Bs
Bed and breakfast inns (B&Bs) offer romantic experiences in small, usually historic, mansions or cottages with live-in owners who manage the property. Rates include full breakfasts but usually no other meals are offered. Although mostly small, Wine Country B&Bs are usually quite luxurious.

8 Camping
The concept of camping in the U.S. usually refers to sleeping outdoors, either in a tent or a campervan with built-in beds. Many state parks have campsites with toilets, water, fire pits, and even showers. Backcountry campsites are usually accessed by hiking, have limited facilities, and require reservations for a fee.

9 Reservations
Book hotels well in advance of your arrival, especially in peak summer months and on major public holidays, such as Easter and Christmas. This is especially true for B&Bs. You can travel around during low season without pre-booking.

10 Out of Season
Wine Country is a year-round destination, but the winter and spring low seasons offer the benefit of lower hotel rates, often as much as 25 percent or more, although some lodgings may require a two-night minimum stay. Wineries are less crowded and you may have easier access to the wine-makers themselves.

Campgrounds at California state parks can be booked at www.reserveamerica.com.

Left **Silverado Resort and Spa** Right **Meadowood Resort**

🔟 Resort Hotels

1 The Carneros Inn
This luxury hotel has 86 country-themed cottages with wood-burning fireplaces. The main lodge is a stylish interpretation of a traditional barn and there's also a spa on-site. ❧ 4048 Sonoma Hwy., Napa, 94559 • Map M5 • 707 299 4900 • $$$$$ • www.thecarnerosinn.com

2 Meadowood Resort
A premium resort hotel, this property is set amid sprawling woodlands and landscaped grounds that include a golf course. There are 15 types of rooms and suites to choose from, and the resort's restaurant boasts three Michelin stars. ❧ 900 Meadowood Ln., St. Helena, 94574 • Map L3 • 707 963 3646 • $$$$$ • www.meadowood.com

3 Silverado Resort and Spa
Offering two golf courses, 10 swimming pools, 13 tennis courts, plus a spa, this resort hotel appeals to active vacationers. Its 435 cottage suites are luxurious and there are fireplaces in half the rooms. ❧ 1600 Atlas Peak Rd., Napa, 94558 • Map M4 • 707 257 0200 • $$$$$ • www.silveradoresort.com

4 The Meritage Resort and Spa
Set amid its own vineyard, this Tuscan-inspired hotel offers tastings in its wine cellar adjoining an underground spa. The 32 guest rooms are equipped with marble bathtubs and flat-screen TVs. ❧ 875 Bordeaux Way, Napa, 94558 • Map M5 • 707 251 1900 • $$$$ • www.themeritageresort.com

5 Silver Rose Inn, Spa & Winery Resort
Surrounded by vineyards, this intimate resort has a winery with a collection of football helmets. Its spa has massage rooms and hydrotherapy. ❧ 351 Rosedale Rd., Calistoga, 94515 • Map K2 • 707 942 9581 • $$$ • www.silverrose.com

6 The Lodge at Sonoma Resort & Spa
A gracious property that combines Tuscan architecture and English décor, the hotel also features the Raindance Spa, which uses local ingredients such as lavender and grape seed in its treatments. ❧ 1325 Broadway, Sonoma, 95476 • Map L5 • 707 935 6600 • $$$$ • www.thelodgeatsonoma.com

7 Fairmont Sonoma Mission Inn & Spa
Amenities at this world-famous resort hotel include the Michelin-starred Santé restaurant and the hotel's renowned spa. The hotel also offers complimentary guided hiking and biking. The deluxe accommodations play on a provincial French theme. ❧ 100 Boyes Blvd., Sonoma, 95476 • Map L5 • 707 938 9000 • $$$$$ • www.fairmont.com/sonoma

8 The Flamingo Conference Resort and Spa
A pet-friendly hotel, the Flamingo welcomes dogs. There's live music and dancing in the lounge on Friday and Saturday, and you can dine alfresco beside the swimming pool. ❧ 2777 4th St., Santa Rosa, 95405 • Map N2 • 707 545 8530 • $$ • www.flamingoresort.com

9 Rio Villa Beach Resort
Just 4 miles (7 km) west of Guerneville, this riverside resort is set in manicured gardens surrounded by redwoods and has its own beach. Bedrooms are comfy and colorful, and many have Jacuzzi tubs. ❧ 20292 Hwy. 116, Monte Rio, 95462 • Map G3 • 707 865 1143 • $$ • www.riovilla.com

10 The Woods Resort
Situated among redwoods overlooking Fife Creek in Guerneville, this resort has rooms in two-level units and free-standing cottages that surround a swimming pool. ❧ 16484 4th St., Guerneville, 95446 • Map G3 • 707 869 0600 • $$ • www.rrwoods.com

Price Categories

For a standard, double room per night (with breakfast if included), taxes and extra charges.	$ under $100
	$$ $100–$200
	$$$ $200–$250
	$$$$ $250–$300
	$$$$$ over $300

Left **Villagio Inn & Spa**

🔟 Spa Hotels

1 Auberge du Soleil
Located on a hillside overlooking Napa Valley, the Auberge du Soleil has accommodations with gleaming wooden floors, hearths, luxury linens, and plush robes and slippers. Their restaurant is excellent and the spa offers signature treatments. 🕾 180 Rutherford Hill Rd., CA 94573 • Map L3 • 707 963 1211 • $$$$$ • www.aubergedusoleil.com

2 Calistoga Ranch
This one-of-a-kind spa hotel makes the most of its woodland environs with 48 guest lodges tucked away in the forest. It has hot soaking tubs over a creek, and the spa specializes in organic treatments. 🕾 580 Lommel Rd., Calistoga, 94515 • Map K2 • 707 254 2800 • $$$$$ • www.calistogaranch.com

3 Kenwood Inn & Spa
The 29 guest rooms in this Tuscan-themed villa have Italian-inspired décor, with sconces, and chandeliers and sponge-washed beige walls. The spa uses grape seed products in its treatments. 🕾 10400 Sonoma Hwy., Kenwood, 95452 • Map K4 • 707 833 1293 • $$$$$ • www.kenwoodinn.com

4 Milliken Creek Inn & Spa
Canopy beds, fireplaces, and gorgeous chocolate and white furnishings highlight the 12 suites at this Napa Valley spa hotel. The spa offers treatments in garden gazebos. 🕾 1815 Silverado Trail, Napa, 94558 • Map M5 • 707 255 1197 • $$$$$ • www.millikencreekinn.com

5 Napa Inn & Spa
Housed in two ornate Victorian mansions, this B&B also has a spa offering various specialty massages and exfoliations. They serve a gourmet breakfast and the property is within walking distance of downtown Napa. 🕾 1137 Warren St., Napa, 94559 • Map M5 • 707 257 1444 • $$$ • www.napainn.com

6 Hyatt Vineyard Creek Hotel and Spa
The Hyatt's rooms are elegant and feature modern appointments such as flat-screen TVs. It has a sculpture garden, fitness center, an outdoor swimming pool, and the Le Carre Spa offers treatment packages. 🕾 170 Railroad St., Santa Rosa, 95401 • Map J3 • 707 284 1234 • $$$$ • www.vineyardcreek.hyatt.com

7 Dr. Wilkinson's Hot Springs Resort
This motel has a spa famous as the birthplace of Calistoga's signature hot mud bath. The motel has varied accommodations, including five rooms in a Victorian mansion furnished with period pieces, plus a heated indoor pool. 🕾 1507 Lincoln Av., Calistoga, 94515 • Map K2 • 707 942 4102 • $$ • www.drwilkinson.com

8 Villagio Inn & Spa
An Italian-themed spa hotel, Villagio has a large swimming pool set in formal Mediterranean-style gardens. The spa is huge and the hotel's 112 rooms have wood-burning fireplaces. 🕾 6481 Washington St., Yountville, 94599 • Map L4 • 707 944 8877 • $$$$$ • www.villagio.com

9 Hotel Healdsburg
This trendy hotel has a gourmet restaurant and a spa with Jacuzzis, a fitness center, and an Olympic length pool. Furnishings in the guest rooms include teak platform beds with goose down comforters, and bathrooms with poured-concrete counters. 🕾 25 Matheson St., Healdsburg, 95448 • Map H2 • 707 431 2800 • $$$$$ • www.hotelhealdsburg.com

10 Euro Spa & Inn
This intimate hotel in downtown Calistoga offers 13 cottage-rooms, each with a gas-fired hearth and whirlpool tub. The spa uses volcanic ash and grape products in its treatments. 🕾 1202 Pine St., Calistoga, 94515 • Map K2 • 707 942 6829 • $$ • www.eurospa.com

Left **Farmhouse Inn** Right **Churchill Manor**

🔟 Historic Hotels

1 La Residence
Dating from 1870, this ivy-clad hotel has a redwood shingle exterior. Down comforters, wood-burning fireplaces, and flat-screen TVs provide a homey coziness to the 26 spacious guest rooms. ✆ *4066 Howard Ln., Napa, 94558 • Map M5 • 707 253 0337 • $$$$ • www.laresidence.com*

2 La Belle Epoque
This gracious Queen Anne Victorian mansion has sumptuous period furnishings. With just 6 rooms and a honeymoon suite, it exudes intimacy. The owners host a nightly wine reception, and there's also a spa. ✆ *1386 Calistoga Av., Napa, 94559 • Map M5 • 707 257 2161 • $$$ • www. labelleepoque.com*

3 Churchill Manor
Elegant antique furnishings, a gorgeous ambience, and an enchanting rose-garden setting define this deluxe getaway, set in a Georgian stately home. The owners pamper guests with a three-course breakfast. ✆ *485 Brown St., Napa, 94559 • Map M5 • 707 253 7733 • $$$$$ • www. churchillmanor.com*

4 Ledson Hotel
Standing over Sonoma Plaza, this historic hotel has just six rooms, individually decorated in gracious yesteryear fashion. Antique wooden beds and chandeliers are combined with modern amenities such as whirlpool tubs. Three rooms overlook the plaza. ✆ *480 1st St. E., Sonoma, 95476 • Map L5 • 707 996 9779 • $$$$$ • www.ledsonhotel.com*

5 Sonoma Hotel
Also located on Sonoma Plaza, this 16-room hotel maintains its original Italian stained-glass windows. Many of the individually furnished rooms have cast-iron antique beds. The Girl & The Fig restaurant is here. ✆ *110 W Spain St., Sonoma, 95476 • Map L5 • 707 996 2996 • $$ • www.sonomahotel.com*

6 Swiss Hotel
With just five guest rooms, this hotel dates back to 1840 and has been in the same family for four generations. Modernized behind the original façade, it is elegantly furnished and has a popular Italian restaurant with garden patio. ✆ *18 W Spain St., Sonoma, 95476 • Map L5 • 707 938 2884 • $$ • www. swisshotelsonoma.com*

7 Dawn Ranch Lodge
This pet-friendly, century old ranch hotel occupies 15 acres (6 ha) of forested property beside the Russian River. Lodging is in cozy old chalets and cottages. Its Roadhouse Restaurant is one of the most popular eateries in the region. ✆ *16467 River Rd., Guerneville, 95446 • Map G3 • 707 869 0656 • $$ • www.dawnranch.com*

8 Raford Inn
Located near the Russian River and Healdsburg, this Victorian inn overlooks vineyards. The six lovely rooms are each named for medicinal plants and furnished with antiques. ✆ *10630 Wohler Rd., Healdsburg, 95448 • Map H2 • 800 887 9503 • $$$ • www.rafordinn.com*

9 Madrona Manor
Set in a mansion built in 1881, this romantic inn has 22 luxurious rooms with the feel of a plush European country hotel. Its restaurant draws diners from afar, and the Dry Creek Valley setting is perfect for exploring local wineries. ✆ *1001 Westside Rd., Healdsburg, 95448 • Map H2 • 707 433 4231 • $$$$$ • www. madronamanor.com*

10 Farmhouse Inn & Restaurant
A charming hotel located in the countryside near the Russian River. Choose from rooms in a modernized barn or cozy garden cottages, with contemporary furnishings. There's also a pool, spa, and gourmet restaurant. ✆ *7871 River Rd., Forestville, 95436 • Map H3 • 707 887 3300 • $$$$$ • www.farmhouseinn.com*

Price Categories

For a standard, double room per night (with breakfast if included), taxes and extra charges.

$	under $100
$$	$100–$200
$$$	$200–$250
$$$$	$250–$300
$$$$$	over $300

Left **Gaige House**

🔟 Bed and Breakfast Inns

Old World Inn
Lavish mahogany paneling and natural stone fireplaces grace this B&B, furnished in eclectic fashion. It offers healthy gourmet breakfasts, complimentary wine, a wine-and-cheese evening reception, and divine chocolate desserts. 🔊 *1301 Jefferson St., Napa, 94559 • Map M5 • 707 257 0112 • $$$ • www.oldworldinn.com*

Candlelight Inn
Housed in a 1929 Tudor mansion shaded by towering redwood trees, this inn is set on the banks of Napa Creek. The 10 rooms are individually furnished, and have whirlpool tubs and private balconies. 🔊 *1045 Easum Dr., Napa, 94558 • Map M5 • 707 257 3717 • $$$$ • www.candlelightinn.com*

Zinfandel Inn
This hotel of natural stone evokes a French château, with a lake and hot tub in the garden. Its three antique-filled rooms include the Chardonnay Room, with a stone fireplace and raised ceiling. 🔊 *800 Zinfandel Ln., St. Helena, 94574 • Map L3 • 707 963 3512 • $$$ • www.zinfandelinn.com*

Brannan Cottage Inn
Perfect for exploring Calistoga, this B&B dating from the 1860s has original cottages from Sam Brannan's early

Calistoga resort *(see p14)*. A porch looks over ornamental gardens. Three of the six rooms have four-poster antique beds. 🔊 *109 Wapoo Av., Calistoga, 94515 • Map K2 • 707 942 4200 • $$$ • www.brannancottageinn.com*

Sonoma Creek Inn
Refreshingly modern, with a colorful décor, this reasonably priced B&B adjoins a café and is a five-minute stroll from Sonoma Plaza. Many rooms have patio gardens with fountains. Friendly staff. 🔊 *239 Boyes Blvd., Sonoma, 95476 • Map L5 • 707 939 9463 • $$ • www.sonomacreekinn.com*

Gaige House
Gorgeous, trendy furnishings set this B&B apart from the crowd. Pathways lead through creek-side gardens to 23 Asian-inspired rooms in various styles that include "Zen Suites" with granite soaking tubs. 🔊 *13540 Arnold Dr., Glen Ellen, 95442 • Map K4 • 707 935 0237 • $$$$ • www.gaige.com*

Inn at Occidental
A home away from home, this inn in the western Russian River AVA has impeccable furnishings and family treasures in its sunlit lounge, 16 individually themed guest rooms, and a two-bedroom cottage. Rockers on a shaded terrace overlook an exquisite garden.

🔊 *3657 Church St., Occidental, 95465 • Map H4 • 707 874 1047 • $$$$ • www.innatoccidental.com*

Haydon Street Inn
A Queen Anne Victorian house painted robin's egg blue, this inn has luxurious spa robes, pillow-top mattresses, and free WiFi in all rooms, some of which have fireplaces. The owner, a professional chef, prepares wood-fired pizzas. 🔊 *321 Haydon St., Healdsburg, 95448 • Map H2 • 707 433 5228 • $$$ • www.haydon.com*

Healdsburg Inn
This lovely B&B on Healdsburg Plaza merges sumptuous comforts with modern conveniences. Most rooms feature bare red-brick walls and have fireplaces. The Carriage House rooms have broad balconies. 🔊 *112 Matheson St., Healdsburg, 95448 • Map H2 • 707 433 6991 • $$$$ • www.healdsburginn.com*

Boonville Hotel
With a refined con. temporary décor, this B&B combines simplicity with quirky details: the Studio, for example, has corrugated metal walls. All four rooms have spacious decks. The hotel's restaurant Table 128 *(see p101)* is well known. 🔊 *14050 Hwy. 128, Boonville, 95415 • Map B3 • 707 895 2210 • $$$$ • www.boonvillehotel.com*

Streetsmart

Left **Andaz** Right **Honor Mansion**

TOP10 Boutique Hotels

Andaz
This relatively modern hotel has 141 stylish guestrooms and suites. Soaking tubs for two and 42-in (107-cm) flat-screen TVs are highlights. The outdoor terrace is a great place to unwind after a day of wine touring. ◎ *1450 1st St., Napa, 94559 • Map N6 • 707 687 1234 • $$$$ • www.napa.andaz.hyatt.com*

Napa River Inn
This pet-friendly hotel in the heart of the Napa River project has rooms in three buildings. Those in the Embarcadero Building have flat-screen TV's over the fireplace and river-view balconies. ◎ *500 Main St., Napa, 94559 • Map P6 • 707 251 8500 • $$$$ • www.napariverinn.com*

Solage
Set in lovely grounds, with lawns, lavender, and oak trees, plus contemporary sculptures, this boutique hotel offers cottage studios with white, green, chocolate, and cream color schemes. Facilities include a spa and a Michelin-starred restaurant. ◎ *755 Silverado Trail, Calistoga, 94515 • Map K2 • 707 226 0800 • $$$$$ • www.solagecalistoga.com*

Bardessono
Zen-inspired architecture and an eco-friendly design highlight this suave hotel, where outdoor showers in the 62 tastefully furnished suites bring you closer to nature. Dogs are welcome. ◎ *6526 Yount St., Yountville, 94599 • Map L4 • 707 204 6000 • $$$$$ • www.bardessono.com*

Napa Valley Railway Inn
Three antique cabooses and six rail cars have been converted into bedrooms with large windows and skylights at this one-of-a-kind hotel, within walking distance of The French Laundry (see p59). ◎ *6523 Washington St., Yountville, 94599 • Map L4 • 707 944 2000 • $$ • www.napavalleyrailwayinn.com*

Bungalows 313
Tuscan-styled bungalows in an English-style garden prove a great combination at this six-room B&B. Comforts include top-class linens, fluffy cotton robes, and designer toiletries. Fresh pastries and healthy granola breakfasts are served. ◎ *313 1st St. E., Sonoma, 95476 • Map L5 • 707 996 8091 • $$$ • http://bungalows313.com*

Honor Mansion
This romantic yet expensive boutique B&B has its own boccie and tennis court, plus croquet and putting green. Choose from three accommodation options: suites furnished with antiques in the 1883 Victorian mansion, garden cottages, or one of four oversize Vineyard Suites. ◎ *891 Grove St., Healdsburg, 95448 • Map H2 • 707 433 4277 • $$$$$ • www.honormansion.com*

Hotel Les Mars
This hotel is the most expensive in Wine Country, with sublime furnishings such as Louis XIV armoires and other choice European antiques. It also has a lap pool and spa. ◎ *27 North St., Healdsburg, 95448 • Map H2 • 707 433 4211 • $$$$$ • www.hotellesmars.com*

H2 Hotel
Chic city styling and a sleek 21st-century design are the draws of this four-story hotel on Healdsburg Plaza. Rooms have minimalist décor and exotic bamboo-wood floors, and there's a creek-side swimming pool plus outdoor lounge bar with fire pit. ◎ *219 Healdsburg Av., Healdsburg, 95448 • Map H2 • 707 433 7222 • $$$$ • www.h2hotel.com*

DuChamp Hotel
Set amid its own olive groves and vineyards, this hotel has six cabana-style poolside cottage suites with minimalist yet deluxe furnishings. It is dog-friendly by prior arrangement and staffed part-time only. ◎ *421 Foss St., Healdsburg, 95448 • Map H2 • 707 431 1300 • $$$$$ • www.duchamphotel.com*

118

Price Categories

For a standard, double room per night (with breakfast if included), taxes and extra charges.	**$** under $100
	$$ $100–$200
	$$$ $200–$250
	$$$$ $250–$300
	$$$$$ over $300

Left **Sugarloaf Ridge State Park Campground**

TOP 10 Self-Catering and Camping

Long Valley Ranch
Set on a 800-acres (324-ha) ranch, Long Valley rents two beautiful, two-to-six-person cottages with walls of glass, kitchens, minimalist furnishings, and patios with mountain vistas. ◐ Off Hwy. 101 near Ukiah, (c/o 2501 Robinson Creek, Ukiah, 95462) • Map C2 • 707 895 3979 • $$$ • www.sheepdung.com

Calistoga RV and Campground
At the Napa County Fairgrounds, this campsite is fully set up for RVs, with water, electricity, sewers and dump station. WiFi service plus showers and restrooms are also offered. ◐ 1601 N. Oak St., Calistoga, 94515 • Map K2 • 707 942 5221 • $ • www.calistogacampground.org

Westin Verasa
This large all-suite hotel has gorgeous contemporary styling. The La Toque restaurant is a true gourmet experience, but guest rooms feature state-of-the-art kitchenettes and kitchens anyway. ◐ 1314 McKinstry St., Napa, 94559 • Map P5 • 707 257 1800 • $$ • www.westinnapa.com

Sugarloaf Ridge State Park Campground
Catering to tent-campers and to RVs and camper-trailers, this state-run campground is around the Sonoma Creek meadow at 1,200 ft (300 m). The camp has drinking water and flush toilets. ◐ 2605 Adobe Canyon Rd., Kenwood, 95452 • Map K4 • 707 833 5712 • $ • www.parks.ca.gov

The Other Place
Sensational valley and mountain views are to be had from the four beautifully furnished cottages of this ranch. Each has a wood-burning stove, telephone, TV, and WiFi. The property has hiking trails. ◐ Off Hwy. 128, Boonville, 95415 • Map B3 • 707 895 3979 • $$$ • www.sheepdung.com

Alexander Valley RV Park & Campground
Most RV and tent sites in this campground have their own fire pits, and the site has WiFi, cable TV hookup, plus flush toilets and a convenience store. It is run by the Dry Creek Rancheria Pomo Indians. ◐ 2411 Alexander Valley Rd., Healdsburg, 95448 • Map H2 • 707 431 1453 • $ • www.alexandervalleycampgrounds.com

Cloverdale KOA Wine Country Campground
Set amid 60 acres (24 ha) of forested foothills in the Alexander Valley, this RV and camping site also has wooden cabins with pine-log beds and bunks, and more comfortable cabins with kitchens. There's also a basketball court, video arcade, and WiFi. ◐ 1166 Asti Ridge Rd., Cloverdale, 95425 • Map G1 • 707 894 3337 • $ • www.winecountrykoa.com

Armstrong Redwood Regional Park Campground
Armstrong Redwoods park has picnic tables, restrooms, and BBQ grills. The campsites are at the adjacent Austin Creek State Recreation Area. ◐ 17000 Armstrong Woods Rd., Guerneville, 95446 • Map G3 • 707 869 2015 • $ • www.parks.ca.gov

Burkes Canoe Trips Campground
Outdoor enthusiasts get to camp beside the Russian River, or inland beneath a redwood grove. Hot showers and flush toilets are offered. The office sells firewood and ice. ◐ 8600 River Rd., Forestville, 95436 • Map H3 • 707 887 1222 • $ • www.burkescanoetrips.com

Liberty Glen
Situated on a ridge with views over Lake Sonoma, this campsite has showers, restrooms, plus hiking and bike trails. Minors must be accompanied by an adult. ◐ 3333 Skaggs Springs Rd., Geyserville, 95441 • Map H1 • 707 431 4533 • $ • www.russianrivertravel.com

General Index

Index

Acknowledgments

Author Christopher P. Baker has contributed to more than 200 publications worldwide and is winner of the 2008 Lowell Thomas Award as the Travel Journalist of the Year. He has authored several other DK guides and promotes himself at *www.christopherbaker.com*.

Photographer Robert Holmes

Additional Photography Andrew McKinney

Fact Checker Carolyn Patten

At DK INDIA

Managing Editor Madhavi Singh

Editorial Manager Sheeba Bhatnagar

Design Manager Mathew Kurien

Project Editor Vatsala Srivastava

Project Designer Neha Dhingra

Assistant Cartographic Manager Suresh Kumar

Maps
Base mapping supplied by U.S. Geological Survey, National Geospatial Program Cartographic Production John Plumer, JP Map Graphics

Picture Research Manager Taiyaba Khatoon

Senior DTP Designer Azeem Siddiqui

DTP Designer Rakesh Pal

Indexer Andy Kulkarni

Proofreader Indira Chowfin

At DK LONDON

Publisher Vivien Antwi

List Manager Christine Stroyan

Senior Managing Art Editor Mabel Chan

Project Editor Alexandra Whittleton

Designer Tracy Smith

Cartographer Stuart James

Senior DTP Designer Jason Little

Production Controller Erika Pepe

Revisions Team Rebecca Flynn, Bharti Karakoti, Hayley Maher, Carolyn Patten, Susie Peachey, Lucy Richards, David Tombesi-Walton, Conrad Van Dyk, Sophie Wright

Picture Credits

Placement Key: a-above; b-below/bottom; c-centre; f-far; l-left; r-right; t-top.

Photography Permissions

Dorling Kindersley would like to thank the following for their assistance and kind permission to photograph at their establishments:

Castello di Amorosa, Clos Pegase Winery, Culinary Institute of America, Cyrus Restaurant, Beaulieu Vineyard, Francis Ford Coppola Winery, The Himalayan Café, The Hess Collection, Healdsburg Museum, Husch Winery, Lachryma Montis, Korbel Champagne Cellars, Robert Louis Museum, Schramsberg Vineyards, Sharpsteen Museum, Sonoma County Museum, Sonoma State Historic Park, Spring Mountain Vineyard, V. Sattui Winery, Zin Restaurant & Wine Bar.

Works of art have been reproduced with the kind permission of the following copyright holders:

© Peanuts Worldwide, LLC: Charlie Brown 7cr, 25tc; Snoopy 44ca, 76c, 80tr.

The publisher would like to thank the following for their kind permission to reproduce their photographs:

ALAMY IMAGES: Danita Delimont 36bl, /John Alves 6clb, 111tr; Lonely Planet Images/Jerry Alexander 46tl; Chuck Place 60tl; ZUMA Press, Inc. 95tl.

ANDAZ HYATT HOTELS: 118tl.

AUBERGE DU SOLEIL: 68tr.

BAYLINK: 106tr.

BENZIGER FAMILY WINERY: 83tl.

CARPE DIEM: 74tr.

CELLARS OF SONOMA: 84tl.

CHURCHILL MANOR: Jumping Rocks 116tr.

CORBIS: National Geographic Society/W. Langdon Kihn 34tr; Galen Rowell 43cl; Max Whittaker 83tr.

CALIFORNIA STATE PARKS, 2011: Bob Young 119tl.

CULINARY INSTITUTE OF AMERICA at Greystone: 16bc.

FARMHOUSE INN & RESTAURANT: 116tl.

GAIGE HOUSE: 117tl.

GETAWAY ADVENTURES: 2tr, 48tr, 94tl.

GETTY IMAGES: Staff / David McNew 108tl.

THE GRANGER COLLECTION, New York: 34tl, 34cl, 35tr.

THE HESS COLLECTION: 3bl, 6cla, 8br, 9cr, 10tl, 10cl, 11cl, 11cr, 38hr.

THE HONOR MANSION: 118tr.

KENWOOD INN & SPA: 62tr.

MEADOWOOD NAPA VALLEY: 62tl, 114tr.

MURPHY'S IRISH PUB: 84tc.

MUSIC IN THE VINEYARDS: Chick Harrity 46tr, 47tr.

NAPA VALLEY BIKE TOURS: 70tl, 106tl.

NAPA VALLEY WINE TRAIN, Inc.: 2tl, 12–13c, 13cra, 13clb, 32–33, 67b.

PHOTOLIBRARY: Age fotostock/ Walter Bibikow 37tr; Alamy/Brad Perks Lightscapes 51tr,/ Gary Crabbe 14–15c, /Hoberman Collection 4–5; Ambient Images/ Thomas Hallstein 56–57; Bios/ Mau/Michel Gunther 1c, 42bl; Jack Goldfarb 111tl; Monsoon Images/ Bob Cornelis 55cla; Ticket/Chel Beeson 108tr.

ROBERT HOLMES PHOTOGRAPHY: 48b.

SONOMA COUNTY FARM TRAILS: 47tl.

SPA SOLAGE: 62b.

VILLAGIO INN: 63tr, 115tl.

WIKIPEDIA: 23tr.

WINE ROAD – NORTHERN SONOMA COUNTY: 46clb, 47br.

All other images © Dorling Kindersley

For further information see: www. dkimages.com

Selected Town Index